The Future Is Now

In this age, when self-help books reach the top of the sales charts, it's apparent that we as humans are no longer content to live our lives without direction. We search for the perfect techniques to improve ourselves. We read books, attend seminars, and spend a period of time each day in pursuit of our quest. These measures are quite effective for some individuals. Others, however, realize that something is missing: they have a goal, and a map to reach that goal, but they're uncertain of the best route to take. They may lapse into despair and do nothing to improve their lives.

Divination provides us with that vital information. It presents us with a view of the direction in which we're heading. By analyzing this information and applying it to our present lives, we can detour around unpleasant destinations and improve the quality of our lives.

As a tool designed to access otherwise unknowable information, divination can play a vital role in conforming our lives to our expectations, dreams, and desires. It can assist us in learning the lessons that we haven't yet mastered, thus smoothing the path that we tread into the future.

Scott Cunningham

About the Author

Scott Cunningham learned about Wicca while still in high school, and practiced elemental magic for over twenty years. The author of more than forty books, both fiction and non-fiction, Cunningham was a much-loved writer whose classic book, *Wicca: A Guide for the Solitary Practitioner*, introduced generations of young witches to the Craft. The continued popularity of Cunningham's books on Wicca and natural magic is a testament to the power and truth of his writings. More than ten years after his passing, Scott Cunningham is still an iconic and highly regarded figure in the magical community. His books on Wicca are considered classics, and his writings continue to inspire and inform those new to the Craft.

Divination
for Beginners

Reading the Past, Present & Future

Scott Cunningham

Llewellyn Publications
Woodbury, MN

Second Edition
Sixteenth Printing, 2021
(Formerly titled *The Art of Divination,* published by Crossing Press, 1993. Reissued by Crossing Press as *Pocket Guide to Fortune Telling,* 1997.)

Book interior design and editing by Connie Hill
Cover design by Adrienne Zimiga
Cover photo © Doug Deutscher
Interior illustrations by Kate Thomsson (pp. 1, 73, 163), and
Kevin R. Brown (p. 187). *Universal Tarot* cards, © 2000, reproduced by permission from Lo Scarabeo.

Library of Congress Cataloging-in-Publication Data
Cunningham, Scott, 1956–1993.
     Divination for beginners : reading the past, present & future / Scott Cunningham
— 2nd ed.
        p.   cm.
     Rev. ed. of: The art of divination. c1993.
     Includes bibliographical references and index.
     ISBN 13: 978-0-7387-0384-8
     ISBN 10: 0-7387-0384-2
     1. Divination.   I. Cunningham, Scott, 1956– Art of divination.   II. Title.
BF1751.C86   2003
133.3—dc21   2003047470

Llewellyn Worldwide does not participate in, endorse, or have any authority or responsibility concerning private business transactions between our authors and the public.
     All mail addressed to the author is forwarded but the publisher cannot, unless specifically instructed by the author, give out an address or phone number.
     Any Internet references contained in this work are current at publication time, but the publisher cannot guarantee that a specific location will continue to be maintained. Please refer to the publisher's website for links to authors' websites and other sources.

Llewellyn Publications
A Division of Llewellyn Worldwide Ltd.
2143 Wooddale Drive
Woodbury, MN 55125-2989
www.llewellyn.com

Llewellyn is a registered trademark of Llewellyn Worldwide Ltd.

 Printed in the United States of America on recycled paper

Contents

Foreword

S cott Cunningham was dedicated to three things: the craft of writing, the Craft of magical living, and genuine loving concern for his readers.

As a writer, Scott kept meticulous notes of his research and never produced less than three complete drafts of his manuscript before sending it off for publication. Often there would be a year or more between drafts so that he could be fully objective in his rewrites. He would check his facts for accuracy and read the manuscript from his reader's perspective to make sure that his instructions were easily understood.

Scott wrote more than thirty books in his short life—some of these were short novels and technical manuals written "for hire" so that he could continue his research and writing for the "real books."

Those real books incorporated his heart and soul. He saw the Universe as magical, and all life as magical. The magical Universe and magical living are two sides of the same coin—for we are part of the magical Universe and when we live in awareness of the magic we live wisely and well.

This is where his love and concern for his readership is revealed. He wanted people to understand that nature is not something "out there," but that we are part of nature and nature is part of us. This gives us both opportunity and responsibility—for not only is all life one, but all of nature is alive and we bring it all together as we live in awareness of the life and love that flows everywhere.

Scott read his author mail—readers asking questions and revealing their personal problems. He took every letter seriously and took them to heart in shaping his writing. He was particularly concerned for younger readers and beginners, trying to live with magical awareness in a culture that predominantly sees nature as mere raw material or even as "the enemy" to be crucified on a cross of materialism.

It is the very fact of this unity between the world out there and that "within here" that makes the art and science of divination possible. In reading cards, or stones, or patterns in clouds, or in interpreting symbols found in dreams or in objects, we are opening the doors of perception to this wider reality where even past and future time are no longer separated from our awareness.

This book was among Scott's last and is a survey and introduction to various kinds of divination. It is a beginning that lets you find the particular kinds of divination that most appeal to you, that let you feel the magic, and that let you communicate with the real world where questions have answers.

It is my hope that you will find this just the first step in the wondrous journey of a magical life.

Carl Llewellyn Weschcke
Publisher, Llewellyn Worldwide, Ltd.

Acknowledgments

The author wishes to express his thanks to the following individuals:

To Vinny Gaglione of Spellbound (New Jersey) for his invaluable contribution of several Italian divinatory techniques.

To de Traci Regula, who gave me access to her personal library.

To Marilee Bigelow, for a discussion concerning certain divinatory systems involving candles and other techniques that we used ten to fifteen years ago.

To Annella, for her instructions in smoke reading.

To Marlene Cole, for assistance with the Tarot chapter.

To my mother and father, without whom the author wouldn't be.

Introduction

Recent years have seen an explosion of interest and activity in discovering the future. Countless psychic telephone lines are open twenty-four hours a day, and most have no lack of customers. Programs that select runes and I Ching hexagrams have been developed to run on personal computers. Tarot decks have never enjoyed greater popularity or higher sales. Major psychic fairs, which attract hundreds or thousands of attendees eager for a glimpse of tomorrow, are well established in every part of the country.

There can be little doubt that we possess an insatiable curiosity about the future. The motivation for obtaining a glimpse of tomorrow varies with each individual, but the desire itself is as old as human consciousness and our perception of time.

Modern technology may have adapted ancient forms of fortunetelling (today termed for legal purposes "psychic entertainment"), but the old ways are still in use by many individuals who wish to be personally involved in discovering their potential paths. This is one of the greatest values of divination: we needn't go to a diviner—we can be diviners ourselves.

In our relatively short history as a species, we've always been riddled with questions, anxieties, and hopes regarding tomorrow. Though in many ways animals and plants are far better predictors of certain occurrences, such as forecasting the weather, humans have developed an amazing array of techniques designed to penetrate the veil that divides today from tomorrow. We also use divination to make difficult choices, to gain a clear picture of the past, and to examine our present lives.

This ageless art has been known by many names. Non-practitioners may refer to it as "fortunetelling" or "soothsaying," both of which are sometimes considered to be derogatory terms. Most experts in these ancient arts simply use the term *divination*, and define themselves as diviners.

This book is a complete guide to the art of determining your past, present, and future. It is written from a viewpoint almost unique in works of its kind, for the author does not accept that we live according to a divine plan (thus allowing us to change the future), We do not need to be psychic to discover our past, present, and future. Anyone can practice divination and receive important information, and this book outlines many methods for doing just that.

Part I consists of an overview of the subject as well as a survey of the importance of divination in the ancient world. Also included are techniques of symbolic thought; the nature of the illusion that we call time, and a workable plan to alter an unwanted future.

Part II contains detailed descriptions of a wide range of divinatory techniques, each grouped by the tools or techniques used to perform them. Many of these utilize natural forces such as water, clouds, smoke, fire, and the movement of birds.

Part III is a brief introduction to more advanced techniques of divination.

The first appendix lists over seventy techniques of divination gathered from all times throughout the world. An annotated bibliography directs the interested reader to sources of further information.

Divination for Beginners is a practical guide to a very practical art. This information is presented to the public with the express intent of providing techniques for seeing possible futures, answering questions, and offering assistance in making difficult decisions. It is based on over two decades of research and practical experience. Though we cannot guarantee the success of any of these techniques, it seems unlikely that they would have survived for five millennia if they weren't effective.

Divination is not a step backward into the days when we were largely ruled by superstition and misunderstanding. On the contrary, true understanding of the forces at work creating our lives requires careful thought and a reconsideration of many of the curious concepts that we hold dear.

There is no destiny or fate. No higher being determines our life plan. This is almost totally in our hands. As a tool that provides otherwise unknowable information, divination can be a powerful ally in reshaping our lives and bringing them into line with our hopes and desires.

Search the past. Examine the present. Look into the future. Only then will you be prepared to fully participate in this great adventure that we call life.

Part I

Aspects of
Divination

1

Beginnings

The earth, the air, the chaos and the sky,
The seas, the fields, the rocks and mountains high
Reveal the truth.

Lucan

D ivination is the practice of determining the unknown by the manipulation and observation of tools recognized by their users as possessing the ability to provide such information.

The ancient art of divination has never lost its popularity. Even today, in our largely materialistic world, we perform age-old rites to discover the shape of the future. In its many forms, divination is as much a part of our lives as it was in the ancient world.

The practice of foretelling the future through the use of tools predates history and so we have no record of the first culture that acted upon its desire to peer into tomorrow. Perhaps the earliest forms consisted of gazing into lakes, watching the smoke rising from cooking and heating fires, and observing the shapes of clouds. In preliterate times all such phenomena were invested with spiritual energies,

3

and it seems logical that it was to these that our ancestors turned for glimpses of tomorrow.

In the great cultures of the past, divination was usually linked with religion. The deities, it was believed, were willing to provide hints of the future if they were given the opportunity to do so. This was provided to them by the presentation and use of specific tools, which the deities manipulated to provide specific responses. The earliest diviners thought that divination revealed the will of the deities. The future, they thought, was unchangeable.

After many centuries of practice, however, it became obvious that this concept could easily be challenged. Why did some events revealed in predictions never occur? Weren't the deities in total control of human life? Some cultures answered such questions by altering their definition of divination. Rather than revealing a fated future, divination provided glimpses of possible future events. The future could be altered by human action. Thus, divination provided a window into potential tomorrows—not of fate. Negative messages were now considered to be useful warnings, not inescapable messages of future doom.

Today, divination is often defined as a branch of magic. This is untrue. The two practices are entirely different. Divination attempts to discover the past, present, or future, while magic is an active process by which the future is thought to be changed. Though magic and divination can be used together, they are in no way related. Those who claim that they are one and the same have no understanding of either practice, or have their own axes to grind.

How It Works

There are many theories that attempt to explain the mechanism at work during divination, some of which are applicable only to specific forms. In general, however, it is believed that our actions and thoughts produce nonphysical waves of energy that extend into the future, and thus shape it to a certain extent. They produce a map of tomorrow based on our current speed and direction, but many destinations lie upon its surface, and we can change course at any time.

Divinatory techniques examine these energy waves—which may not be consciously known to the diviner—and, by taking them as well as other forces into account, paint a picture of the future—if things continue on the present course for some time.

The tools reveal the unknown information in a wide variety of ways. Some of these (the use of the pendulum or sand divination, for example) seem to rely on the subconscious mind, in which we become aware of these streams, to produce the response.

Others techniques are completely free of our conscious or subconscious control, relying on other forces to manipulate the objects and to produce the prediction. In these forms, which are usually the most reliable, we simply present the tools and allow them to do the work.

The Major Types of Divination

By studying the hundreds of techniques used in cultures throughout history, scholars have divided divination into two basic forms: *operational* and *natural.* Operational divination consists of the manipulation of tools (smoke, oil in water, eggs, dice, pieces of paper, knives, stones, and so on) to determine the future. Such tools are used in specific ways for this express purpose. These represent later developments of divinatory technique.

Natural divination consists of the observation of occurrences in the natural world. A specific time and place is set aside for the express purpose of asking that omens derived from natural physical phenomena present themselves to reveal the future. The casual observation of omens that may unexpectedly occur at any time isn't true divination. Omens must be preceded by a request for information in order to be classified as divination. These are known as *provoked omens.*

Such omens are created by the world around us. The flight or appearance of birds, the behavior of animals, observation of the stars and clouds, the wind's activity, and the sudden appearance of meteors and lightning are some popular forms.

The Divinatory Response

Messages received during divination are known as responses. They usually take one of three forms. The nature of the technique determines the message's form.

The first form produces so-called *binary* responses. The techniques that create binary responses are the easiest to perform and often produce the clearest answers. Questions are asked that can be answered with a yes or a no; hence the term binary. Occasionally, a third option, "maybe," "perhaps," or "no answer" is also included.

The second response consists of the creation of symbols or images. These forms are termed *symbolic.* The divinatory tools (particularly crystal spheres, clouds, fire, smoke, and oil dropped into water) produce symbols that are interpreted in conjunction with the diviner's question. Forms that produce such responses aren't limited to answering specific questions; they can be used to determine the general future. The symbols thus produced are interpreted to provide information such as "it will be a prosperous year," or "expect losses," and so on.

Symbolic responses rely both on the diviner's powers of observation as well as on her or his ability to unlock the symbols' inner meanings. Generally speaking, only symbols familiar to the diviner will appear, and this enhances the probability of a successful interpretation. (See Chapter 4, Symbolic Thought.)

The value of techniques that produce binary responses is obvious: no such interpretation is necessary. Both of these forms, however, can produce satisfactory results if used with the proper attitude. (See Chapter 3, The Fine Art of Divination, for further information.)

The third type of divination produces what we may term *selective* responses. A number of likely future events are written on pieces of paper, leaves, stones, or on other tools. These are then manipulated (placed in a windy spot, chosen at random) to provide the most likely prediction.

Divination Isn't Psychic Awareness

Many of the processes at work during divination are little understood. However, one fact is clear: true divination doesn't consist of the use of psychic abilities. It doesn't rely on a person's ability to tap into a bank of knowledge usually unknown to the conscious mind. Because of this, anyone, psychic or not, can successfully practice divination.

It can certainly be argued that our psychic minds may be at work during some techniques—that they examine waves of future energy and then relate them (through symbolic responses) to our conscious mind. No such awareness can be at work during techniques that produce binary or selective responses, yet all three systems can produce insightful answers.

Some diviners still believe that higher beings manipulate the tools or, alternately, place symbols within them for us to see. This, the ancient view, may or may not be accepted according to the diviner's spiritual beliefs. Such a belief isn't necessary, for even nonreligious persons can satisfactorily perform divination.

Why Is the Past of Importance?

Some question the need to examine the past to discover the future. This is based on the assumption that we know everything about our pasts because we've lived them.

Why, then, do so many divinatory techniques focus on both the past and the future? Most Tarot spreads (see Chapter 18) include a placement for a card that symbolizes the past as well as the future. Magic mirrors and other tools are used to illuminate the past, especially to see the circumstances surrounding a crime that has been committed at an earlier time.

The fact remains that divination has always been used for this purpose. The explanation of why is rather simple: every day, we're building our futures. Every decision that we make affects tomorrow. When we're faced with a difficult situation, we may ask ourselves, "Why?" The answer often lies in the past.

Though most of us can remember our pasts, we may not be able to make the conscious connection between past and present. We're incapable of seeing that we reap the fruits of our actions. If, yesterday, a man decided to sit on train tracks for twenty-four hours, and is then run over by the train, he's feeling the effects of his past decision.

If we make unwise choices we'll suffer because of them. Deciding not to take an important medication may result in a severe relapse this week. If we allow another person to steer us away from our goals and dreams, we may find ourselves living an unfulfilling experience bereft of happiness. Moving to a town that's flooded every year during heavy rains will probably make our shoes wet. Though these are simple examples, the fact remains that many of us are simply unable to link past actions and the present state of our lives.

The past also affects the future, for the streams of energy not only follow us, they race on into the future, continuing to mold our lives. Becoming aware of these past streams can not only answer questions concerning our present lives, but can also provide hints of the future. Therefore, examination of the past can be of great importance in divination.

Divination remains a mysterious art. Perhaps this is part of its appeal. Scientific inquiry and education have largely stripped our lives of mystery. Though the purpose of divination is the clarification of the future, the manner in which this is achieved is highly romantic and evocative. This may explain why divination has never lost its popularity during the 5,000 years of its practice.

2

Divination in the Ancient World

Virtually every culture has practiced divination. This process wasn't limited to a few countries; it was a worldwide phenomenon. Divination was in common use in Japan, India, Tibet, China, Southeast Asia, Polynesia, Melanesia, Micronesia, the Americas, Africa, Australia, New Zealand, and throughout Europe.

My omission of Egypt in the above list isn't an oversight. Few early records of divination (much less of the actual techniques employed) exist. The greatest number of records date from Graeco-Roman times, a late period in Egyptian history, and by then Egyptian techniques were well mixed with Babylonian, Greek, and Roman practices. Perhaps the early Egyptians kept such information committed to memory, secret, and not to be recorded in hieroglyphics or on temple walls.

In this chapter we'll examine the techniques used in ancient Babylon, Rome, ancient Germany, and Tibet. Those used in a few other cultures are discussed in Appendix 1: A Dictionary of Divinations.

Babylon

In ancient Babylon and Assyria divination was considered to be the most important of the sciences. A multitude of forms were created and used to provide insights into a future that was usually, in that place and in that time, filled with uncertainty and hazard. Fortunately, we have some ancient sources of information regarding divination in Babylon and from these we can gain a picture of rites that were practiced in virtually all Middle and Near East cultures.

The Diviner

A special class of temple priests performed nothing but this ancient practice. The earliest records that we possess of these diviners date from approximately 1900 B.C.E. (Before Common Era), which indicates the great antiquity of Babylonian divination.

These potential diviners, called *baru*, were chosen from the upper social classes and enjoyed great privileges. Priestesses of this type (who usually limited their workings to dream interpretation) also existed.

Baru had to be free of all blemish. No limbs, fingers, or toes could be missing; the eyesight had to be perfect; the teeth sound. The overall impression had to be that of a healthy individual. Even pimples were reason enough to exclude a student from study.

And study they did. These classes were quite lengthy (all forms of schooling were of importance in ancient Babylon) and, during them, the student learned every aspect of the divinatory arts so that all could be used whenever needed. After completion of study, students underwent an initiation and then either set up shop in a temple or were retained by a ruler to be on call for advice concerning the future. They were true professionals.

No army would march out to battle without at least one of these diviners in their company. At times they may have also acted as generals. It couldn't have been neater or more appropriate: the person who performed divination then used them to decide battle plans.

Old clay tablets urge the baru to be totally honest at all times. A countercheck (that is, a repetition of the first divination) was always performed to ensure accuracy. At times a third repetition also followed. If all were in agreement, the diviner made a statement based on the responses. If, however, these counterchecks were conflicting, the diviner was instructed not to make any statement whatsoever, because the will of the gods hadn't yet been determined. Perhaps, when the oracles were silent, the same divination would be performed at a later time. Some diviners were devious enough to attempt to convince their employers that negative omens were actually favorable, but such baru probably didn't last long in a professional capacity. Absolute truthfulness was another essential quality in the professional diviner.

Divination in General

Divination, as previously stated, was used as a method of discovering the will of the deities. Following a national disaster, diviners were quite busy asking the deities, through various rites, why this had occurred. Divination was also relied upon to predict future troubles. Thus warned, the diviner (or the client) could make offerings or perform protective rites to circumvent the foreseen disaster. If, however, the future appeared bright, the diviner or client would pray to the deity in thanks and place appropriate offerings on the altar.

Many techniques were used (although most of these have been lost). In fact, the only remaining information stems from a few Akkadian clay tablets that record such rites from the Old Babylonian period. Undoubtedly, however, similar divinatory techniques were in use in Sumer, the great culture that preceded Babylon.

Some practices were reserved for kings, others for the upper class, and there were also those to which the poor (who couldn't afford the usual necessary sacrifices) reverted.

Divinatory techniques imported from other nations found a fertile ground for further development and usage in Babylon. On the other hand, many Greek and Roman methods were directly based on Babylonian workings. As the techniques were passed on and continuously practiced throughout the ancient world, some became quite complex. In a way, divination grew to be considered an exacting art.

Forms of Divination

The diviners observed the flight of birds, poured oil or flour into water, burned special woods and studied the smoke thereby created, provoked omens, cast the lots, induced dreams, and studied the entrails of sacrificed animals, among other techniques.

Some of the minor forms of divination seem rather strange to our eyes: to discover if the diviner was loved, she or he buried a frog in the sand and left it for seven days in the sand. Then the bones were dug up and cast into a river. If the bones sank, the emotion was hate—if they floated, it was love.

A curious divination consisted of sprinkling water three times on the forehead of an ox lying on the ground. The anointed animal would then react in one of seventeen ways, each of which foretold a specific event. For example, if the ox snorted and rose to its feet, the diviner (or the client) would attain all desires. If it snorted and didn't rise, the desire wouldn't be fulfilled.

Divination with Oil

Lecanomancy, divination with oil, seems to have developed very early in the Middle East, and continued to be used by many of the cultures that were otherwise busy conquering each other. Indeed; similar rites are still in practice today (see Chapter 17: Other Forms of Divination for specific instructions in this art).

In this practice, the baru sat with a bowl of water resting on his crossed legs. A small quantity of oil was poured into the water. The various movements and shapes of the oil as it floated on the water's surface indicated ill or good. This was performed to discover a possible birth, future battles or periods of peace, the prospects of recovery for the sick, possible business success or failure, even an appropriate mate.

A similar form entailed pouring flour into water. There is less information available about this practice, but it seems likely that the flour, by quickly sinking or floating, by forming into globules, or even by its movements creating recognizable shapes provided a response.

Divination with Smoke

Libanomancy, the art of reading the smoke from smolder-ing incense or fires, was also an ancient Babylonian prac-tice, but not much information remains. Only two ancient clay texts describing this technique have survived the thou-sands of years that separate its earliest practitioners from our culture.

We do know that the censer was held on the diviner's lap. An aromatic plant material (usually cedar shavings) was tossed onto the live coals in the censer, and the future was divined by the smoke's behavior. (See Chapter 9: Fire, Candles, Smoke, and Ash for more information.)

Lecanomancy and libanomancy were considered to be the precious legacy handed down to later diviners by the famous Emmeduranki of Sippar. These forms were far less costly than many others, such as *extispicy*, in which the in-teriors of sacrificial animals were examined to provide the needed response. Even the poorest citizen could occasion-ally afford to hire a diviner to perform divinations such as these.

Omens

Perhaps the most popular form of divination was the provocation of and interpretation of omens. Though the Babylonians observed omens at all times, they clearly dif-ferentiated between provoked and natural omens. Both were considered to be highly accurate predictions of future events, and extant tablets contain hundreds of possible omens and their interpretations, described in the most ex-haustive detail.

Omens were derived from all phases of life, from birth to death. Events in cities, the construction of houses, unusual sounds, puddles, the movement and behavior of animals and insects—the list is endless.

A few specific rules were used in interpreting every type of omen. Anything that occurred on the left was favorable; on the right, unfavorable. Movements (by animals, insects, birds, shooting stars, etc.) were observed according to the same interpretative rules.

At times, whole series of omens were provoked and observed. These could be conflicting, so the diviners followed these rules: if most of the omens were positive and only a few were negative, the prospects were favorable. If the greater number were negative, unfavorable.

Ordeal by Water

Another form of Babylonian divination consisted of an ordeal. A person suspected of a crime was thrown into a river. If she or he sank, guilt was assured. If, however, the water refused to allow the person to sink below its surface, innocence had been proven. Water, a sacred commodity in the middle of a desert, would never punish an innocent person. (The parallels to the common medieval and Renaissance European practice of *swimming* suspected witches are clear, though in this later form a person's guilt was assured *if she or he floated*; innocence could only be proved if the person sank to the bottom of the lake or river. Either way, death was usually the result. The Babylonian criteria seems far more humane.)

Casting Lots

The most famous of the ancient divinatory arts consisted of the casting of lots. The Sumerians used wooden sticks, the Assyrians used clay dice, and Babylonians used bone dice.

Lots were cast to elect public officials, but were also used to divine the future. In every instance, it was accepted that the lots were controlled by the deities, who, through their manipulation of the dice or sticks, revealed their will.

Astrology and Astronomical Phenomena

Many believe that astrology was created in ancient Egypt. All surviving records, however, prove that Mesopotamia was its birthplace. When I speak of Babylonian astrology, however, I'm not referring to the modern practice of astrology. Indeed, most present-day astrologers would shudder at the notion that astrology be included in a work concerning divination. Still, the earliest extant records show that this ancient practice grew out of the observation of the positions of the planets, their appearances, the phase of the moon, and other astronomical phenomena that were thought to affect human life in Babylon. In other words, astrology was originally a form of omen observation.

It is not surprising that astrology developed in the Middle East. Skies were usually free of clouds. Little light shone from nearby cities and towns. Thus, an incredibly detailed view of the heavens was possible. Centuries of observation led to the development of the Babylonian calendar (which, admittedly, wasn't as accurate as that produced by the Egyptians). This was one of the important first steps in the recognition of the zodiac—a necessity to astrology.

The earliest, crudest forms of astrology consisted of the observance of signs seen in the sky. These were considered to be straightforward omens. However, the Babylonians didn't believe that the stars determined the fate of humans. Rather, they believed that the deities moved the stars and planets around (or altered their appearance) to provide warnings or other messages of future events.

In approximately 1700 B.C.E. a series of tablets was written, containing over 7,000 celestial omens and observations, illustrating their importance to the early Babylonians. The range of planetary, star, and lunar omens from these and other texts is staggering.

From these observations, astrology evolved as a tool for determining the future. The earliest surviving example of what we would recognize as a personal horoscope (that is, a chart of the heavens created from birth data together with an interpretation) dates from 410 B.C.E. This document reveals that, at the moment of this child's birth, the moon was in Libra, Venus in Taurus, Mars in Gemini, Jupiter in Pisces, Saturn in Cancer, and so on. This development was only possible after the discovery of the zodiac, which seems to have taken place in about 700 B.C.E. Most of the earliest charts were rather tersely interpreted; many simply stated that the future looked favorable. Others indicated poverty or a long life in the child's future. Most horoscopes seem to have been cast for kings and officials—they weren't available to everyone.

The complete story of the development of astrology as a science of revealing future trends has filled several books, but this short section should serve to illustrate its importance in old Babylon.

Prevention Rituals

As previously stated, omens were often considered to be warnings of impending doom, on a personal or a larger scale. Thus, the Babylonians evolved a number of both simple and complex purification rites called *namburbi*, designed to avert the evil and appease the responsible deity, which would change the future.

Special priests expert at exorcism seem to have performed some (but not all) of these rites, particularly in response to omens of impending disaster that affected the entire city. The namburbi included lengthy prayers as well as some rather extraordinary acts. Omen texts occasionally include both the presage as well as the necessary purification ritual to prevent its manifestation, if it was negative.

For example, if upon waking on New Year's Day someone sees a snake emerge from a hole and the serpent seems to look at the person, their death was ensured within the following year. To avert this catastrophe, the sleeper was directed to shave their head and cheeks. Sickness would still result for a period of three months, but the forewarned person would eventually recover, having successfully altered the revealed future.

In ancient Babylon, then, divination was a cherished practice. The diviners were quite serious in their activities and the efficacy of all forms seems to have been unquestioned. There were some dishonest diviners, but it was the operators, not the techniques themselves, that were sometimes mistrusted.

Most cultures throughout history have performed various forms of divination. In ancient Babylon, however, this art rose to a great height, to which it will probably never again ascend.

Rome

The most widely quoted of the Roman writers on the subject of divination are Livy, Aeschylus, Aeneas, and Cicero, but many others made references (in praise or jest) to the practice. There's little reason to doubt divination's importance in the Roman empire.

Roman divination was seen as a method of communication with their gods and goddesses. It was practiced by a wide range of social classes, though there were certainly diviner priests who did little else. Many of these experts were frequently consulted as Rome continued to expand its empire. Omens of the outcome of planned battles were constantly required.

There were many methods, few of which were of local origin. Some were created by their Etruscans forebearers, while others were passed from Babylon to Greece, and hence to Rome. Among these practices were:

- **The ritual creation of dreams** and their subsequent interpretation. After ritual, the person in need of a divine response slept overnight in a temple. The deity appeared in a dream to reveal the needed answer. [Note: this subject is more thoroughly covered in the author's book *Dreaming the Divine*. See bibliography.]

- **The reading of omens.** Like the Babylonians and the Greeks, Romans were inveterate omen-watchers. They classified omens into two types: the provoked, and the unprovoked or natural; that is, those that occurred not in answer to the diviner's supplications but were created by the deities of their own volition.

Omens derived from carnivorous birds were considered to be a most reliable source of such information. At times, a question was asked and the sky was watched for the sudden appearance of birds. Their number, direction of flight, and other factors were observed.

Observing the manner in which sacred chickens ate food was one form of bird augury. Observing ritual silence, the birds were released before piles of food. If they ate, and if the grain dropped from their beaks onto the ground, this was a most favorable omen. If, however, they refused to eat, or scattered the grain with their feet, a dire forecast had been made.

Generals in the field and admirals at sea kept cages of these chickens. A famous account of the use of these birds for divination was preserved by Ovid. The Admiral Publius Clodius, during the First Punic War, was about to attack the Carthaginians. Though he didn't believe in divination, he performed the usual rite before battle: he set out food for the chickens. They refused to eat, thus predicting disaster for Clodius. Angry, he had his men throw the chickens into the sea, stating, "If they won't eat, let them drink." Clodius was defeated: the birds had been right. (This story was viewed as a warning against taking sacred rites in jest.)

Omens were also derived from many aspects of daily life. One that was greatly relied upon was the chance overhearing of a word at unexpected times (as when passing two others engaged in conversation). These words often contained messages far different than their speakers' original intent.

Other omens include changes of the weather; the appearance of meteorites; the behavior of animals; the behavior of the human body (twitching, sneezing, and a forerunner of palmistry); daily home life (such as substances being spilled) and, notoriously, the use of sacrificed animals.

Though the last of these, *extispicy*, was available only to the wealthy, the vast majority of common citizens could perform some type of divination. Because omen observation had a long history, and incurred little or no cost, this was by far the most widely used form among all social classes.

Apparently, no one technique of divination was thought to be more effective than any other. After all, the deities themselves had revealed these methods to humans. Their express reason for doing so was to offer their worshippers tools by which they could communicate with their deities. Thus, as long as the form possessed the patina of great antiquity, it would prove effective.

Problems did sometimes arise among official diviners, but as in Babylon, the fault lay in dishonest humans, not in the techniques they used. Many diviners were forced out of business and potential clients became more careful of their selection of a seer. The writer Artemidorus, in his work on dreams, warned his audience against relying on the multitude of sham fortunetellers and readers that were in business throughout ancient Rome.

Ancient Germany

What is here termed "'Germany" refers to the area from which a people spread across much of Scandinavia and Iceland centuries before the Viking Age. This is an early time, little documented. We're indebted to ancient Roman writers for what little information has come down to us. More is known about the practices of the Vikings, but they represent the last survivors of the original practitioners of these ancient arts, separated from the earliest Germanic times by 900 years, and discussed only in passing.

Divination became so firmly established in what is now known as Germany that the first German national council, held in 743 C.E. (Common Era), warned of the continuing reliance of the German people on divination, despite centuries of Christian dominance. Three hundred years later new laws were passed that forbade the practice of divination.

The early Germanic people saw divination as a means of determining the fate that their deities had allotted to them. In this regard they were in perfect agreement with most other cultures of the time. Tacitus and Julius Caesar both attest to the faith that the Germanic peoples placed in divination. What does somewhat separate early Germanic peoples from other cultures is the apparent complete acceptance of women in the role of diviner, especially in the use of lots. Though much remains murky, we can form a partial picture of the divinatory practices of this ancient people. Perhaps the most commonly used technique was that of casting the lots.

Lots

In this ancient art, a variety of tools are thrown or otherwise manipulated to determine the future. The deities themselves were said to direct the manner in which the lots fell, and from them the future was determined.

According to the Roman writer Tacitus, lot casting usually began with prayer. In later Viking times, this was almost invariably addressed to Odin, who was a master of these arts. We know little of the deities to whom such prayers were addressed in the earliest periods.

The procedure for consultation of the lots was time-honored and rarely altered. Tacitus describes it as consisting of the use of small strips of wood sliced from a fruit- bearing tree. Upon these lots were inscribed various signs. These tools, which seem to have been made afresh for every casting, were then tossed at random onto a white cloth spread out before the diviner.

The diviner offered up a prayer and stated a specific question that needed to be answered. Sitting on the ground, gazing at the sky, the diviner chose at random three of these marked sticks. The response was revealed in the symbols, which were read both separately and in common, with the question in mind. Additional castings were often used to determine the original response's truthfulness.

The later Vikings certainly used a similar method. We know that they marked runes on their staves or sticks. Though the symbols used by the earliest Germanic peoples weren't recorded, it appears likely that they resembled the runes used in later times.

Lot casting was sometimes employed to select the most suitable human victim for sacrifice (from among the collected prisoners of war). Perhaps each potential victim's name was marked on a stave and then one of the staves was selected at random.

In contrast to Tacitus, who said that men usually divined, Julius Caesar wrote that divination was usually performed by women. In Latin they were known as the *matres familiae*. These were usually older women (during this period of hard, short lives, they might be thirty or forty years old). The oracles received from these women were as highly respected as those from men.

In one famous example of lot-casting by women, the ancient leader Ariovistus abandoned a planned attack against the Romans because the divining woman had, through her rite, discovered that no move should be made before the full moon.

Other Forms of Germanic Divination

Other forms include divination by the observation of birds; the behavior of special horses kept for this purpose; duels (between two men, one from each side in a battle, to determine the chances of victory or defeat for both sides); and by other methods. Still, the casting of lots was probably the most favored of all forms.

Tibet

Westerners have always considered Tibet a far-away place, a land of mystery. In a sense this is quite true. Ancient forms of magic and divination are still accepted there as a part of everyday life. (The same can be said for Japan.) Divinatory techniques developed in the past are in common use. Though they may seem alien to our eyes, they've been continuously practiced for untold millennia.

In the following information I use the past tense to discuss Tibetan forms of divination. However, be aware that most of these are still in use, usually hidden from the eyes of the Communist party, but alive nonetheless.

Diviners

Those who practiced divination were collectively known as *mopa*. Though anyone could divine, most mopa were reincarnated lamas called *tulkus*. These persons, through repeated incarnations, had achieved great wisdom and continued to use it in the present life. The Dalai Lama is perhaps the most famous tulku of our time.

Still, if a person desired to learn divination, and set out to do so, she or he could indeed become a mopa. Most of these were elderly persons, especially women, and some became widely known for the accuracy of their predictions. In fact, it wasn't uncommon for a person to travel many miles to seek the advice of a highly respected diviner. Though some practiced only part-time, talented individuals often relied on divination and the casting of horoscopes as their only means of support.

As is the case with diviners virtually everywhere, the job lasted only as long as the predictions were accurate. This sometimes led to the ambiguous manner in which mopa revealed the future. Symbolism was widely used.

Reasons for Divination

Persons from all walks of life turned to divination to settle questions concerning routine matters: business, legal concerns, marriages and births, lost objects, the success of new endeavors, sickness and recovery, and the prosperity of the coming harvest.

Tibetans apparently believed that it was the mind that created the responses received during divination. This view is consistent with their concept that all is created within the mind. However, this belief in no way lessened the value of the responses.

Forms of Tibetan Divination

Many techniques produced symbolic responses. Others were far more direct. Most divinatory techniques bear some resemblance to the methods used by other cultures. This clearly demonstrates that humans often turn to similar objects (or to natural phenomena) to produce predictions.

Tra, scrying, consisted of gazing into a mirror, the sky, or a lake. Through concentration and chanting, the diviner created images of the future. These images were, at times, actually seen by others, though they were the product of the diviner's mind. In common with Western methods of gazing (see Chapters 10, 11, and 15), the response was usually symbolic. It demanded a person with great interpretive abilities to unlock its message.

Tring-Ba consisted of the use of a *mala*. This is similar to a rosary, though it has no Christian connotations. Indeed; rosaries were in use hundreds of years prior to their adaptation by the Catholic church.

The mala consists of a string of 108 beads. Used in daily spiritual rituals, it was an ideal tool with which to predict the future.

The mala was held between the hands as the diviner silently asked her or his question. The diviner then randomly changed her or his grip on the mala. A number of beads remained between the hands. These beads were then ritually counted in a number of ways. One of the commonest of these consisted of counting them off by fours. Beginning at the right, four were counted, then four to the left, and so on. Eventually a number of beads between one and four would be left. This number determined the oracle's response. This procedure was repeated three times.

The possible combinations of numbers obtained during the three repetitions were also read together. Ancient texts list hundreds of these combinations and their meanings for specific questions.

Another form of divination, by the use of a lamp filled with butter, resembles techniques of fire observation used around the world. The brightness of the flame; its shape and color, and the behavior of the wick were carefully watched for omens of the future. No symbolism was used here; the flame directly revealed the response.

Tibetans also performed divination using dice and by the observation of birds. Crows were considered to be among the most reliable species.

3

The Fine Art of Divination

Virtually anyone can successfully practice divination. With practice and a sincere acceptance of the underlying theories, we can gain information concerning the past or future and (perhaps of equal or greater importance) analyze our present situation.

Divination is an eminently practical art. A few complex techniques require years of study, but most of those presented in this book can be performed with no such exertions. With a few exceptions, the tools used in divination are readily available at little or no cost.

Before we discuss the techniques themselves it is necessary to examine some of the finer points of divination. The following five chapters provide a wealth of information geared toward successful divination. Using the information presented here will only increase the veracity of the responses.

The Appropriate Attitude

First, your attitude toward the practice itself is of the utmost importance. If you perform divination in fun, or to entertain others at gatherings, chances are that incorrect messages or nothing at all will come through—precisely because you're not taking the process seriously. This is simple logic: why should an oracle accurately respond when the diviner possesses no genuine interest in its messages?

Doubt, in the earliest stages of your divinatory work, is perfectly understandable. You lack the experience that will eventually convince you of divination's genuine ability to assist us with our lives. Once you've grown comfortable with the proceedings, and have gained true insights into the future through their use, release this doubt and replace it with the firm knowledge that divination is a workable and remarkably effective art.

Your attitude toward the process may be spiritually based. If you're a spiritual or religious person you might view divination as a process that reveals messages sent by a higher being. This can help to erase all doubts concerning its viability, even in the earliest stages of your work, for divination can be seen as a supplication for guidance and advice.

Even if you're not a particularly spiritual person (and you don't have to be to practice divination), it's important to respect the tools and techniques that you use. They are somewhat mysterious and, because of this, deserve our respect.

Keep in mind that divination has frequently changed the course of history. It has halted battles, toppled rulers, designated the location for the founding of cities, and has been directly or indirectly responsible for the ways in which countless individuals have shaped their lives.

Simply respect the art, the tools used to practice it, and the responses thus received.

Selection of a Suitable Form

This book contains detailed instructions for performing over 100 different types of divination. With so many available options, it may be difficult to decide which method to use. Ideally, one will immediately draw your attention, and this may well prove to be the most effective method. Always listen to your intuition. If you enjoy plants, *botanomancy* may be right; if you play cards, *cartomancy*. If you've always felt a fascination with fire, this may be the most accurate tool that you can use.

By way of example, I've always been attracted to water in all forms: rivers, lakes, oceans, fountains, and even sprinklers whirling on the lawn of my suburban childhood home. When I first began practicing divination I immediately used those aspects that rely on water. Though I've worked with many other systems, those involving water have been most effective.

If no one system immediately attracts you, work with a number of techniques until you find the one best suited to your needs and temperament. This should produce the most accurate responses. (See Chapter 6: Determinations.)

There's no reason to limit your workings to one particular form. Indeed, in matters of great importance you may wish to ask the same question using two or three different methods and compare the answers.

The Question

As mentioned in Chapter 1, most forms of divination produce responses in one of three ways: "binary" (a yes/no response), "symbolic" (the creation of images or symbols), and "selective" (the technique chooses a specific prediction). All of these can be used to answer questions. Divination isn't always performed to answer specific questions. Indeed, readings may be used to provide general insight into the future. Still, most. of us need responses to specific queries regarding the future. Questions are thus of the utmost importance.

Questions should be carefully formulated. You should be earnest in your desire to receive a response. Clear questions will produce clear answers. Use common sense. Asking something like "Will I go to Cleveland or Portland next spring?" cannot be answered in a binary system.

The above question actually contains three queries: "Will I go to Cleveland?" "Will I go to Portland?" "Will I go there in the spring?" When using a system that's limited to yes or no answers, each possible future event or choice must be separately questioned.

Below is a typical series of questions, used in this case to discover the whereabouts of a lost set of keys. The responses are gained through the movement of the pendulum (see Chapter 19: Other Forms of Divination).

Q. Are my missing keys in the house?

A. Yes.

Q. Are my missing keys in the bedroom?

A. No. (If a positive response is received, the following question would be skipped.)

Q. Are my missing keys in the living room?

A. Yes.

Q. Are my missing keys in the trash can?

A. No.

Q. Are my missing keys in the couch?

A. No.

Q. Are my missing keys behind the couch?

A. Yes.

Such a series of questions is often necessary to cover all possible options. These have been in use since ancient Babylonian times in which the official diviners often spent hours listing every possible future occurrence of concern to the king.

The necessity of repeating the technique several times to obtain the needed information may seem to be a great deal of work, but actually requires little time. However, many techniques provide explicit answers with only one repetition.

Such questions may be written, stated aloud, or thought. Different systems use different methods. Unless instructions specifically state otherwise, use what feels best.

Repetition of Divination to
Answer the Same Question

In some cases, the response may be unclear, or you may otherwise be unsure of the oracle's response. When this happens it's best to repeat the divination three times. This provides the technique the ability to formulate a more comprehensible response, and may lessen the possibility of misinterpretation on your part.

Preparation for Divination

Though many forms of divination were designed in ancient times to be used at a moment's notice, some required ritual preparation: prayer, offerings, the burning of incense and aromatic woods, bathing, donning special garments, and so on. None of this is necessary today, but they may be used prior to divination if desired.

The rationale for such practices is clear. They calm the diviner and allow her or him to concentrate on the question to be asked. Ritual is a process, usually of conscious origin, that accomplishes a specific need. In divination, this need consists of preparing the diviner for the coming act.

If you feel the need for some kind of predivinatory rite, one of the most effective is also one of the most accessible. Sit quietly for a few moments. Breathe deeply. Don't strain your lungs, simply allow a slightly longer period of time for each inhalation and exhalation. Think your question. Then move on to the actual technique itself.

Most diviners agree that, if circumstances allow, it's best not to eat a large meal directly prior to divination, as this is thought to *desensitize* the diviner; to make certain forms such as gazing more difficult to successfully perform. Still, even this precaution is never necessary, and divination should be used when needed.

No special costume is needed: no mystical headgear, no sacred jewelry, no star-covered robe. Some techniques were traditionally practiced naked (such as divination through mirrors), but this is not necessary. It's mostly of symbolic value: unadorned and unafraid, the person is ready to receive the response.

Appropriate Times For Divination

Some ancient writers recommended specific moments, based on the position of the planets, as being ideal for forecasting the future, but this is a highly complex art and doesn't necessarily produce better results. Divination can be performed at any time of the day or night, in any season. Some claim that better results are obtained during the waning of the moon or at the time of the full moon. Certainly the night may be preferred as there are fewer distractions to the process (though this would obviously preclude those techniques that require sunlight).

Interpreting Symbolic Responses

If you've used a method of divination that produces images or symbols, interpret them immediately after they're received. In this fine art the diviner must rely on her or his intuition. Though symbols can be astonishingly clear, others need close scrutiny. (See Chapter 4: Symbolic Thought for a further discussion of interpretation.)

Try to think in symbolic ways during this important aspect of the divinatory arts. Open yourself to the answer. Keep your question in mind. If you still encounter problems, repeat the divination; the symbols may be clearer.

A Lack of Response

At times you won't seem to receive any response at all. Alternately, some forms of divination include an option of "no answer is possible at this time." When this occurs, don't despair.

A lack of response isn't always an indication of failure. It may simply mean that too many energies are at work at the present time to make an accurate prediction. When this occurs, try the technique again at a later time.

This seems to be a form of a built-in safety device. Receiving no response is far better than receiving an inaccurate answer. If desired, use divination to determine why no response can be produced. This in itself can be quite illuminating.

When Divination Fails

As stated in the beginning of this book, every decision, thought, and action may dramatically alter the course of our lives. The waves of energy that we radiate, and those of others who are in our lives, can change the future. Thus, sometimes a reading may produce a response that doesn't seem to come true.

Many forms of divination produce warnings. If a reading indicates that you'll be involved in a car accident on a specific day, and you don't get into a car that day for the express reason of avoiding such an accident, you've changed the future—and, thus, have voided the prediction. This isn't a sign of failure of the chosen technique but of our ability to change our own futures. (See Chapter 7: Changing Your Future.)

While some forms of divination are certainly open to error in interpretation (not only of the foreseen events but also of their time frames), those with which the practitioner is most comfortable should produce reliable responses.

Reasons for experiences to the contrary include: the technique isn't the most successful for the diviner; the technique isn't the best for the specific situation; or the technique wasn't repeated at least twice to provide further, clarified information. Vague questions may also be the culprit. Switch systems if necessary. Always ensure that your question is properly formulated.

Reading for Others

Once we've discovered divination, and have reaped the many benefits that we can gain from its usage, it's only natural to want to assist our friends with the same techniques—particularly those who are experiencing problems and who have come to us for some type of assistance.

While it's understandable that you may wish to help, performing divinations for others isn't recommended until you've gained proficiency in at least one system. By proficiency, I mean that you've successfully performed the divination on several occasions and have worked sufficiently with symbolic thought. Nothing is more disconcerting to someone who comes to you for help than watching the diviner surreptitiously consulting a book to find the meaning of a response. The only exception to this is the I Ching.

On a related note, we may want to use these techniques to discover our friends' futures without their knowledge. While this may be a symbol of our concern for their well-being, it's also an invasion of privacy. In this age of wiretaps, computer files, even machines that display the number from which a telephone call is originating, the future may well be one of the few private areas that we have left. It simply isn't ethical to perform divination concerning other persons without receiving their prior and explicit consent.

If you do gain proficiency, and others ask you to perform divination in their name, keep these things in mind:

- You are not a professional diviner. Be prepared for the occasional mistake.

- Realize the very great burden that you're assuming. You're placing yourself in a position of power over another human being. Never joke or jest during the divination itself. Maintain the appropriate attitude. Think carefully before you speak. A possible trap is falling into the role of oracle. Some persons will believe everything that you say and feel the need for frequent sessions. When reading for such persons, limit sessions to once a week or month so that they don't become dependent on your advice. You have a responsibility to those who come to you.

- Never charge for such work unless you set yourself up as a reader, which certainly isn't recommended, and may cause problems with local officials.

- Search for positive signs or responses. If you see accidents ahead, don't say "You'll break your leg on Tuesday."

- Realize that symbolic forms of divination may be more difficult to interpret when performed for others. If this is the case, simply describe the response to the friend who has consulted you, and let him or her solve the puzzle.

- Finally, and perhaps most importantly, inform the friend that the future isn't carved in stone. Explain that a negative future can be avoided by making changes today. Dismiss all ideas of fate and divine will, and put their minds at ease.

Reading for others can be a satisfying practice, but only if such advice is kept in mind.

The Dangers of Reading for Yourself

It isn't wise to perform a divination with preconceived notions. If you think "this will tell me that I won't lose my boyfriend," you'll be likely to see just that, ignoring negative clues or discounting the advice of binary methods.

The conscious mind and the subconscious mind can cause us to either deliberately or unknowingly misinterpret a response. This illustrates the importance of clearing your mind of anything but the question directly prior to divinatory rituals. Don't think of your desired answer.

Avoid seeing negative signs as being positive. Don't ignore what seem to be important answers simply because they aren't pleasing to you. To ensure that they continued to receive favors from the king, a few of the diviners attached to the courts of ancient Babylon used the most obscure and twisted reasoning in an attempt to rationalize negative responses as positive. The king always expected positive answers. Don't allow your desires to alter your interpretation of the response.

Additionally, never allow yourself to become totally dependent on divination. This can lead to all manner of problems. We can certainly make decisions based on a number of other sources of information. Divination is simply an additional source—it needn't (and shouldn't) be our only one. Perhaps it's best to reserve it for those questions that are of the greatest importance.

In summary, if you perform divination with a positive, serious attitude, choose the most effective methods, formulate clear questions, interpret the response (if necessary), and don't bring preconceived ideas into the process, you should receive helpful advice.

4

Symbolic Thought

Those of us who possess the ability to read use symbolic thought. After all, what are printed words but strings of symbols, the meanings of which are generally agreed upon? If we're aware of the symbols' meanings we can create an accurate interpretation. A person with no knowledge of English would gaze uncomprehendingly at these words, for she or he would be in the dark concerning their correct symbolism. The same would be true of illiterate persons.

Symbolism has probably been a part of the human existence since the earliest times, long before the alphabet. However, humans used the most graphic form of symbolism to communicate with the spirit world and with animals.

The earliest evidence can be found in the decorations applied to cave floors, walls, and ceilings in many parts of the world. These symbols were stunningly realistic representations of food animals and stylized human figures. Though a bison may not have been physically present, there was one on the wall—symbolically.

Eventually, humans realized that they could use pictures as a means of communication with other humans. The earliest form of written speech was little more than small, stylized sketches of common objects (known as pictographs). Pictographs were used to represent physical objects, such as animals, the sun and moon, household tools, trees and plants. Grammar had yet to be developed, so these pictographs were simply strung together to form rather obscure sentences. They were ideal, however, for creating lists, which don't require grammar.

Some of the earliest pictographs found to date originated in Mesopotamia before 3000 B.C.E. As the centuries passed, their symbolism grew. Eventually, these symbols became ideographic, that is, they could represent both the physical object as well as qualities associated with it. Thus, a pictograph of the sun meant the orb as well as light. A plant referred to the plant itself and food; a star to the sky as well. (Written Chinese still consists of ideograms; it has no alphabet.) In time, the greater symbolism attached to each pictograph grew far too confusing. The next step was the formation of a simpler method of recording information.

Pictographs were soon altered and stylized. In Mesopotamia, a pictograph of the sun became a series of wedge-shaped marks that formed a highly stylized symbol of the sun. As cuneiform (as this form of writing is termed) progressed, the symbols no longer obviously resembled the objects, forces, or concepts that led to their origins; thus, special training in understanding and creating these signs was required. It was necessary to see them in symbolic ways. With the invention of cuneiform, humans were well on their way toward the use of more complex symbolism.

As early cultures advanced, symbolism was freed from the constraints of alphabetic designs. Ideals, natural forces, human emotions, and deities attained physical symbolic forms. Much of this form of symbolism was found in early religious rituals. A plow represented a grain deity; a helmet, a god or goddess of war. A shell could represent the ocean, food, travel, and freshness. Many cultures created groups of such symbols for use in conversation, literature, and ritual.

Our own culture possesses many symbols. A heart is widely seen as a modern symbol of love, as is a ring placed on a finger. Colors have great symbolic value: red, for example, means "stop" or "pay attention." Some containers of poisonous substances still bear a skull and crossbones. As we grow from infancy to maturity in our culture we're directly taught to recognize and to correctly interpret these symbols.

We're taught that symbolism has its place, but that spoken and written language is the ultimate form of communication. Consequently, our ability to interpret symbols has waned. We even think in language: "I don't want to go. I don't want to go!"

This isn't symbolic thought. Symbolism can certainly be expressed in language, both spoken and written, but symbolic thought consists of the recognition of nonalphabetic symbols and their interpretation. As has been previously mentioned, this is of vital importance in all symbolic forms of divination.

Once you've seen symbols in the fire, in clouds, in a crystal sphere, even in a cup from which you've drunk tea, it's usually necessary to interpret them. This is impossible without thinking in a symbolic way.

Sometimes in-depth thought isn't necessary in interpreting divinatory responses. If you've asked whether you should continue on your present course, and you see an eight-sided figure attached to a straight stick, the meaning could well be "stop"; that is, change your life and alter your course. However, the production of even this simple interpretation requires the ability to view symbols in relation to the question and to find the common link.

Some forms of symbolic responses may require more work. This process is made much easier by following the techniques below.

Look for Symbols

This may seem obvious, but many of us aren't used to this practice. If all you see in the clouds are clouds, you're not involved in symbolic thought. Don't see the symbols as consisting merely of their outer forms. Avoid being dazzled by their physical structures. Expand your consciousness.

Interpret According to Your Symbolism

Trust your instincts. If, for example, you see a dog while cloud-gazing, allow its inner meaning to come to you. If you think of dogs as loyal and faithful friends you may view their appearance as positive signs. If, however, dogs have always terrified you, you may well have a different interpretation. If your dog companion has recently passed on, this, too, may affect the interpretation.

Most books of fortunetelling include long lists of symbols and their correct interpretations. This is especially true of tea-leaf reading. This type of information is usually of little use, for it isn't linked with our personal symbolic systems. Using it to predict the future can cause errors in interpretation. Such information can be safely ignored.

How do you discover the meanings of symbols? There's no need to worry about this. The divinatory tools that you use will usually produce symbols that speak to you. Think about them for a while after they appear. Interpret them in conjunction with the question, if any.

Give yourself permission to think in a symbolic manner. Our hard-science, super-realistic society has discouraged the use of this faculty. Only writers, theorists, and artists are allowed to do so, and even these persons are usually berated for wasting time.

If Difficulty Arises

Occasionally, the symbols produced may not seem to have any specific meaning. If you asked about your future love life, and all that you saw during divination was a frog, you might wonder if the technique had failed you.

It may be necessary to extend symbolic thought to greater depths. What do frogs do? They live near water. They hop around. This symbolism may mean that you won't settle down with a specific person for some time.

Additionally, no system of divination will produce accurate responses every single time. Too many factors—those waves and ripples of energy mentioned in Chapter 1—are constantly at work. This uncertainty of the future may be revealed by the appearance of nonsensical symbols. If you find that you simply can't make a connection between the symbol and your question, you have two options. Either perform a second divination to clarify the response, or wait and repeat it at a later time.

An Exercise to Develop Symbolic Thought

This exercise can be used at any time for this purpose. It requires only a few moments for concentration. No matter where you are (at work, at a bus stop, at home, in the woods), study the things around you. Your eyes may fall on a coffee pot. Use symbolic thought—what does coffee symbolize? Wakefulness? Morning? A friend who visits every day for a cup? Or, you might see a pencil. Communication? Problems with communication in a relationship? Creativity? You're not performing divination here; you're honing your ability to think in a symbolic manner.

Performed several times a day, this exercise will prepare your mind for symbolic thought when the need arises during divination. It's so quick that it shouldn't intrude into your everyday life.

Some people* have difficulty, not in interpreting symbols, but in recognizing them at all. If you experience this, practice one form of symbolic divination on a regular basis. Allow no more than ten to fifteen minutes for each session. As you retrain your consciousness you'll eventually become aware of the symbols.

Fortunately, not all forms of divination produce symbolic responses. The binary (yes/no) and selective systems are usually quite straightforward. If you have difficulty with symbolic thought, and if you have specific questions concerning the future, you may wish to rely on these techniques for the time being.

Symbolic thought is the birthright of every human. In a sense, it represents an older form of human behavior in which we reach back through time to an age when there were two worlds: the physical and the symbolic.

5

The Nature of Time

O ur senses tell us that time exists. We see seeds sprout, trees lose their leaves; the sun rises and sets. We watch as a baby is born and grows to maturity. Clocks tick off seconds, minutes, and hours, and calendars keep track of the passage of days and months and years.

In some systems of Asian philosophy, time is seen as an illusion (as is everything else). It is useful for ordering our lives, and we can go bed at night secure in the knowledge that upon waking it won't be ten years earlier but a day later. Time is viewed as a convenient tool whereby we can organize our existences, but it doesn't truly exist.

Even when viewed at the most simplistic level, our perception of time may be somewhat confusing. When you began to read this chapter, it was the present. That moment is now in the past. You're currently experiencing a new present, and the future is but a moment away.

Time isn't a universal law. It isn't a physical phenomenon such as gravity. Time consists of our perception of what seems to be a natural phenomenon.

Any book that discusses divination would be incomplete without a short introduction to some of the theories of time. This chapter offers you a few of the most commonly accepted ideas, determines whether they're supported by the practice of divination, and ends with the most useful of all conceptions of time. Thinking about time in a different way than normal is of importance to the diviner, who can't assume that time moves inevitably from A to B to C. Only in viewing time from a larger, less physically based viewpoint can we be successful in looking into the past, present, and future.

The most common, least metaphysical explanation of time is that it consists of a one-way path or stream. Birth puts us into a ship on this stream. We sit facing downstream, able to see the past and look to either side to gain knowledge of the present but unable to look behind us to see the future. We continue our voyage until we leave this plane of existence. This theory doesn't support the practice of divination. It states that we can never know the future, for it simply hasn't yet happened.

A related theory again sees time as a river or stream. Usually, we float down this river, directing our voyage. Though the strong current impels us to move forward, we can, through effort, travel upstream and revisit where we've been, or jump ahead for short periods to see what lies around the river's bend. This allows us the flexibility of perceiving the future, but it still sees time as a linear phenomenon. Thus, it isn't particularly suited to divination.

Yet a third concept of time is that of a book. We can start reading at the beginning and continue on through the end, but it's perfectly possible to look ahead and read how the story ends; that is, to look into the future. This theory is based upon the assumption that the future is already written, and that we can read these words. Though this concept supports the practice of divination, it is dependent upon the concepts of fate and destiny; thus, divination doesn't support *it*.

A fourth concept is almost poetic. Time is a spiral that has always existed. Our lives lead to the center, but the path is already set. We can jump from one part of the spiral to another to see what has been or what will be and then return to the present to live out our lives. This, too, is based on predestination, on fate, and so doesn't fit our definition of divination.

Some believe, however, that time is far more complex than any of these theories. It consists, not of linear (straight) motion, but of motion in all directions; of zigzags and curves and circles and spirals. It's this activity that's responsible for the creation of what we perceive to be the past, present, and future. Time itself is seen as a dimension that intersects with our physical world; that measures it but doesn't in any way control it. It also brings order into our lives. To paraphrase Einstein, time is what prevents everything from happening at once.

In this view, the past, present, and future don't exist and yet simultaneously exist. It is, again, our perception of events as occurring yesterday, today, or tomorrow that provides a structure on which to build our lives.

In Chapter 1, we saw how the energy that radiates from our past and present actions creates our future. Think of yourself as standing in the middle of a large plain. Hundreds of paths stretch out from your position, each representing the past or a potential future. The position that you occupy is the present. We can look down the roads that we traveled to arrive at this time and, by examining them, can determine which of the future paths we'll likely take. This is the process of divination—of finding the most plausible path. However, we are aware that we can alter the future by taking an alternate path. All lead to the same destination: a future present.

As is obvious from the above paragraph, it's virtually impossible to discuss divination without resorting to the use of such terms as "past," "present," and "future." Our perception of time is a valuable ally in our lives, allowing us to view them as linear experiences, even though we know that this isn't so. To return to our earlier image of time, we're standing in the center of all those paths, walking toward that center and traveling away from it simultaneously.

If the information in this chapter seems confusing, realize that few persons (other than philosophers and perhaps physicists) ever dwell on the nature of time. We've been taught that time operates in one specific manner, which allows us to live our lives in a structured manner.

In summary:

- Time is an illusion. However, it's an extremely valuable illusion.

- Today is built on yesterday; tomorrow on today.

- Divination offers a means of reaching beyond the constraints of time; of seeing the past, present, and future.

- The present is in the past; the future is already here.

It isn't necessary to have a Ph.D. in physics to practice divination. Simply alter your definitions of terms such as past, present, and future.

6

Determinations

This chapter consists of two parts. The first part presents a technique useful for determining what may well be the most effective form of divination to use for answering a specific question based on the Tarot.

The second part describes four techniques designed to discover the time frame of an already-received prediction. It is an adaptation of lot casting.

These rites are never necessary to the satisfactory performance of divination. However, they can be used as desired.

To Determine a Suitable Method of Divination

This is a rather odd technique of my own creation that can be used by anyone. Designed to reveal the most appropriate method to answer a question, it relies on the major arcana of the Tarot to provide answers (see Chapter 18 for more information concerning traditional methods of using the Tarot).

In the following technique, the Tarot is used in a manner different from the usual way. You need not have studied and worked with the Tarot to successfully utilize the following technique. The interpretations given below are quite clear. The cards aren't used as symbols of the future themselves (but only point out the most appropriate method of divination to answer a specific question).

In Chapter 3, I stated that one form of divination may seem to be the best for you. At times, however, this might not be possible to practice, or you may wish to utilize an alternate form. This Tarot divination provides a quick and simple method of making such a determination.

First, obtain a Tarot deck. It doesn't matter which version, but never use a deck that others have owned. Remove the minor arcana (the Wands, Swords, Cups, and Pentacles) and set it aside; it's of no use in this technique.

Place the major arcana (the twenty-two remaining cards) face down on a flat surface. Mix the cards with your hands. Ask for guidance in the selection of the best divinatory technique.

Choose one card at random. Turn it over and read, from the list below, the most appropriate method. (Some decks use alternate names for the major arcana.)

0 The Fool: None should be used immediately.

1 The Magician: Crystallomancy.

2 The High Priestess: Moon gazing (either directly or at the moon's reflection on the surface of water).

3 The Empress: Plants and herbs.

4 The Emperor: Knives.

5   The Hierophant: Stones.

6   The Lovers: Roses and apples.

7   The Chariot: The hearing of chance words in public.

8   Strength: Fire, candles, incense, and smoke.

9   Hermit: Omens seen on journeys; *bibliomancy*.

10 Wheel of Fortune: Pendulum.

11 Justice: Birds.

12 Hanged Man: *Dactylomancy*.

13 Death: None should be immediately used.

14 Temperance: Wine.

15 Devil: None should be immediately used.

16 Tower: Casting of lots.

17 Star: Stars, meteorology, provocation of sky omens.

18 Moon: Water.

19 Sun: Candles.

20 Judgement: Fire.

21 The World: Any form.

If you're proficient with the Tarot, some of these attributions may seem strange, but they're only partially based on traditional Tarot interpretations. They're a new method of using an old tool.

To find specific instructions for the performance of any of these techniques, please consult the index.

Determining the Time
Frame of a Response

As we've seen, time doesn't truly exist. Rather, it's only our perception of time as a linear progression of events that exists. These events have an existence independent of our observation, and indeed can be observed in many ways.

However, since we do include such concepts as yesterday, today, and tomorrow in our symbolic vocabularies (or, to put it another way, the past, present, and future), and because much of divination is designed to reveal the future, it's often necessary to place these events in a time frame. Will the omen take place next week? Next month? Next year?

You could, of course, consult many other forms of divination to determine the time, but the methods that follow are easy and may be used if desired.

They have predecessors. One charming version consists of blowing on a seeded dandelion head. The number of breaths required to completely clear it of the winged seeds determines the hours (or days, or weeks as the case may be) until an event will occur. The following methods are useful when dandelions haven't gone to seed.

For Immediate Events

To determine the possible hour of an event, collect fourteen smooth, flat stones of the same size. (Garden shops often carry them.) Paint each stone with one each of the numbers between one and twelve. Allow to dry, turn them over, and repeat the same number on the back.

Paint the thirteenth stone black. Allow it to dry and paint the other side with the same color. Leave the fourteenth stone plain.

When all stones have been prepared and are fully dry, place them in a cloth bag. State your question: "At what hour will such and such occur?" Reach into the bag and remove a stone. If it is one of the numbered ones, this represents the hour. Choose again and ignore all other stones until you obtain the black or plain stone. If the plain stone is found first, the hour will be in the A.M. If the black, the P.M. If either the plain or the black stone is retrieved first, the question can't be answered at this moment.

Within a Week

This requires a different set of tools. Paint the names of the days of the week on seven stones. Add two blank stones, mix them in a cloth bag, ask when, and retrieve one as usual. If you select one of the blank stones, no answer is possible. Otherwise, the stone will reveal the day in question.

Within the Next Few Months

Obtain four stones of the same approximate size. One should be white, one green, one red, and one brown. Mix these up in a small bag or bowl and, with your eyes closed, select a stone at random. Remove the stone and determine the time frame:

White: In one month.

Green: Two months.

Red: Three months.

Brown: Four months

Within a Year

Utilize the same four stones. Mix, ask for specific information concerning the time of the prediction's manifestation, and choose a stone at random.

White: Winter.

Green: Spring.

Red: Summer.

Brown: Autumn.

Some will argue that such techniques may well not be effective, for we do change our futures, and perhaps it's best not to pin down predictions to specific dates and times. However, if they're used to setting a definitive time for a future event, they can provide us with a window of opportunity to take action to alter negative future events, or prepare us for positive occurrences (see Chapter 7). Failure of the event to occur at the predicted time doesn't always indicate a failure of the technique. See this as a demonstration that the future is always in motion.

In any case, countercheck and confirm all of these divinations until you're certain that, based on current information, they're as correct as possible. If you receive conflicting or confusing answers, either try another system or wait for another time.

7

Changing Your Future

One of the commonest misunderstandings concerning
divination is the mistaken belief that it reveals our
destiny. This is incorrect, for the future as seen in divinatory responses can be changed. This was first discovered by
some of the earliest cultures. Even within most religious
doctrines, humans are regarded as possessing free will. We
certainly have the power to alter the future.

As seen in Chapter 2, the Babylonians firmly believed
that they could change a foreseen future through the use of
specialized rituals and prayers to their deities. Similar concepts have been held in a number of cultures.

It would be wonderful if every divination produced positive responses; if each reading revealed future happiness,
peace, fulfilling love, prosperity—in short, a rosy, idealized
future in which nothing negative, harmful, or dangerous
would intrude.

This rarely occurs. Humans are humans. We make mistakes, allow others to guide us down dark roads, rely on

our emotions when we should think, or use our brains when we need to feel. No life is completely devoid of the bumps that lie on the road. Meeting and overcoming these challenges is a part of our daily existence

True, tragedies are usually balanced with triumphs, losses with gains, and broken relationships with more fulfilling ones. Divination has the ability to forecast both joy and pain. It's the latter that will be discussed in the first section of this chapter.

Our futures aren't preset flight plans. We create them with every choice in action that we make.

Karma

Some accept the doctrine of karma, and may wonder how we can escape its effects. Because karma is widely accepted today, it's important to discuss it here from a divinatory viewpoint. How does karma affect the future? This is easily explained if we briefly examine this eastern concept.

Karma is often described as a phenomenon that has a direct influence on our lives. Past actions (especially negative ones) will be returned to us through a mystical process that is little understood. It is an illustration of cause and effect. If we make mistakes, we'll receive lessons in the future that instruct us to avoid such behavior.

These lessons may take the form of challenges that we would otherwise wish to avoid. Some say that the effects of karma are inescapable. Moreover, there are those who state that even our actions in previous lives can return to haunt us in our present existences.

Many persons see karma as a type of universal teacher. We must show up for school and learn correct behavior. According to this view, at least part of our future is predetermined by our own actions.

However, there are lessons and there are lessons. Some individuals use divination (or past-life regression) to reveal these karmic debts. Once they're aware of the problem, they take action. Following the teaching analogy used above, these persons do their homework so that the coming test will be of minimal pain. Though they may be unable to escape the effects of karma, they are able to work with the process.

Karmic lessons may be viewed as the phenomena of the return of energy waves that we radiated at previous moments of our lives. Thus, like our futures, we create our karma on a daily basis. Though we might not be able to fully escape being faced with these lessons, we can certainly alter our current behavior to avoid future challenges, tragedies, and other painful situations by acting positively and living a positive life.

Karmic lessons may be seen in some predictions of the future. Prepared and forewarned; we can take action now to minimize their impact and yet learn our lessons.

The Stumbling Block of Fear

Fear is an intense human emotion. It's also one of the most irrational, harmful, and imprisoning of all human feelings. It can literally destroy a person's life, whether the fears are grounded in fact or not. In divination, fear often arises from ominous messages concerning the future.

Fears that are created in this manner are dangerous, for they may actually assist the warning to manifest. Subconsciously or consciously, we give life to the prediction through fear. Sitting around the house worrying about the future is one of the best ways to prove that divination produces genuine responses. We don't need this kind of verification.

It is apparent that we need to release such fears, to give them no power. Failure to do so will negatively reprogram our energy waves. A lack of positive action is the worst possible avenue in such situations.

Many techniques have been developed to combat this problem. In her classic work *Positive Magic* (Phoenix, 1981), author Marion Weinstein terms one such process as "interceding." Weinstein suggests releasing fear through a simple statement. Though she specifically relates this technique to advice provided by the I Ching, it can be successfully used with warnings produced by any technique (169–170).

If you suffer from fear of the future, you may wish to write a short affirmation. It could be something like the following:

> *I take responsibility for my actions. I release guilt*
> *concerning the past and fear concerning the future.*
> *Fear of the future has no role in my life. I have the*
> *power to change my future.*

Such a simple statement, repeated several times a day, may be a boon to releasing fear. Once this has been accomplished (and you may need to perform a divination, perhaps with a pendulum, to determine if you've been completely successful), it's time for positive thought (or focusing) and positive action.

Action and Thought to Prevent Negative Future Events

There is no time like the present to begin reshaping your future. The exact methods of accomplishing this rely largely on the nature of the warning received, but the following advice may be used with minor adaptations to deal with all types of warnings.

One word of advice: warnings concerned with important matters received during divination should always be double- or triple-checked to ensure that no error in technique or interpretation has created the response.

1. Retrain your mind. Focus on a positive future. True, other types of problems may occur, but never think about the negative response. Block it out of existence; don't consider it as an inescapable part of your future.

2. Use further divinations to determine the most effective method of creating the change. Techniques that produce yes or no answers are favored here, for there's no room for erroneous interpretations (unless the divinations are incorrectly performed).

3. Work at correcting one problem at a time. If you're faced with many warnings, choose the most negative. Once you've successfully achieved the necessary changes (determined through divination), take a rest. Begin to work on lesser problems at a later date.

4. Act in accordance with your need. If, for example, you've foreseen that a planned move will cause you heartache, illness, or financial loss, take steps now to change your plans if you wish to avoid this future.

Or, you may see trouble concerning a relationship. If so, reexamine your feelings toward the person. Increase communication. Lay it all out on the line. Some relationships need hard work to be emotionally fulfilling for both parties. Don't allow the warning to be manifested.

If sickness is foretold, change the patterns of your life. Get regular, nonintensive exercise. Eat low fat, low sodium, whole, and healthier foods. Cultivate a positive outlook on life. Because stress has been clinically proven to cause illness, reduce stress by all available methods. Break life-draining habits.

After releasing fear, use affirmations on a daily basis to celebrate the coming positive change as well as to strengthen your conscious and subconscious resolve. These need be no more than one or two sentences; in fact, the more compact they are, the easier they are to memorize.

Some find it difficult to accomplish genuine change. Many of us are stubborn. We don't like to change our plans; we become set in our ways. Such feelings must be released if we wish to be successful at altering our futures. Be more flexible. See other possible avenues of actions as challenges, not problems.

5. Take responsibility for your life as it is now. Realize that no higher being has predetermined its course. Steer toward calmer waters. Also assume responsibility for the lengths to which you've allowed others to adversely affect your life. Forgive yourself for your mistakes, release guilt, and get on with the process of creating your future.

The Nature of Such Techniques

Some argue that these methods rely solely on the powers of our subconscious minds. This is only half of the picture, true. Positive thinking and affirmations can indeed change our lives, but the energy waves from present actions can cause much greater changes, and positive thinking can't affect many events. People who believe in this concept are usually of the opinion that all divinatory messages are created in the subconscious mind, and that this form of consciousness can also be used solely to alter the future.

This theory has severe flaws. Here's just one example: saying an affirmation every morning and evening won't stop an earthquake or prevent a storm that will cause widespread flooding. However, we can avoid being caught in such disasters by taking physical steps to ensure that we won't be in these areas. In other words, if we're warned of an earthquake or a flood, we can move out of the area to avoid the harmful situation. Thus, positive thinking must always be combined with positive action to affect true and lasting change. It is never wise to rely solely on your subconscious mind.

The energies of those whom we know (socially or in business) can also greatly affect our futures. We all know someone who, upon meeting a new acquaintance or lover, has completely changed her or his life in accordance with the desires of the new companion. Such changes may be positive or negative and, indeed, may well be the stimulus for a received warning.

Positive thinking can't directly affect the energy waves of others with whom our futures have become entangled. If divination reveals that these waves are being negative, it may be necessary to make a difficult choice between continuing the friendship or going off on our own, thus removing their energy waves from ours. The former may be dangerous. Altering our futures can indeed be challenging.

But it's far from impossible. Work at it. Don't surrender yourself to fear. Recheck all warnings to be sure of their veracity. Use positive thinking and positive action in accordance with your needs. End damaging or dangerous relationships. Gain the confidence that you are truly the captain of your soul and the creator of your future. See such concepts as destiny and fate as being the products of fatalistic humans who will take no responsibility for the state of their lives.

Action to Alter Positive Future Events

That said, it may become quickly apparent that some future events revealed by divination, while fairly positive, aren't in alignment with our wishes and desires.

A divination may foretell an impending pregnancy. Some women would welcome such a message. Others would be less than pleased. These messages can be seen as warnings if we don't desire the predicted change.

Such revealed positive future events can also be altered. Indeed; we must shape our lives to match our goals and desires. Some positive actions necessary to change the future are obvious: if the woman described above doesn't wish to become pregnant at this time, she can avoid sex during her fertile times. Alternately, she could choose to use a more reliable form of birth control. In either case, she will have used positive action to change her future.

Other positive omens can be altered in similar ways. Use common sense, act with the firm resolve that creating such change is within your power, and recreate your future.

The techniques described in this chapter may seem obvious. They are. You needn't make offerings or chant long prayers, purify your body and mind, circumambulate sacred trees, or practice other mystic rituals to change your life. It's this emphasis on practicality that enhances the accessibility and usefulness of this system.

If you're involved in a spiritual path, it's perfectly permissible (and perhaps even advisable) to petition your personal deity for support and strength during the process of change. However, don't leave it up to your deity to create these changes. This often produces no change at all.

As you began reading this chapter, you may well have questioned its entire premise. By now, I hope that you've realized the very real power within your grasp: change today and you change your future.

Part II

Techniques

8

Water

Water is a fascinating element. It moistens and fertilizes the land, cleanses the air, washes our cars, flushes impurities from our bodies, provides a surface upon which long journeys may be made, causes plants to grow to feed hungry humans and animals, and carves the landscape into fantastic shapes. Such uses led to the acknowledgement of deities in lakes, rivers, oceans, springs, and in water in all its forms. Even artificially created wells were viewed with reverential awe, and few persons, especially in arid areas, took water for granted.

Water has long been studied to provide omens of the future. Its color, clarity, ebb and flow, temperature, the height of rivers, and the behavior of the seas all provided messages. Bubbles rising to the surface of springs offered clues, as did water rippling on large liquid bodies.

Water is traditionally considered to be a feminine element. Its moist coolness generally symbolizes growth and purification, love and psychic awareness, healing and peace. Due to these and other qualities, it should come as no surprise that water has been and continues to be a popular tool in many forms of divination.

Hydromancy (divination with water) is said to have been created by Nereus, the Greek god of the sea and of all water. A standard method of water divination in ancient Greece consisted of filling a vessel with water at night. Torches were placed around the bowl. Lengthy invocations followed. Finally, a chaste boy or a pregnant woman was seated before the vessel. In reflections on the water's surface, the diviner saw what was to come to pass. Hydromancy, however, embraces several other techniques, all of which utilize this most useful of elements.

Water Gazing

The simplest of these is known as gazing or scrying, in which water is used to create symbols of the future. To perform this ancient rite, pour water into a blue ceramic bowl. Ask your question. Sitting with your back to the light in a darkened room, gaze into, but not at, the water. (Some people add a few drops of blue food coloring or ink to the water to darken it; this is particularly useful when using a light-colored bowl.)

As with a crystal ball (see Chapter 13), the water may cloud. Eventually you may begin to see symbols within its cool depths. Make note of any such symbols. When no further symbols are seen, begin the process of interpretation.

Some water gazers prefer to have a candle's light reflected on the water's surface. Others take the bowl outside on a cloudless night and, capturing the moon's reflection, divine by its appearance on the water. All three of these techniques can be used.

A method related to water gazing involves wine. Pour wine into a clear glass. Place a candle behind it and light it. Sitting before the glass, ask your question (if any), gaze into the illuminated wine, and search for symbols to appear. This is known as *oinomancy*.

Sycphomancy is defined as the use of cups or glasses in divination (as in the above technique). It is of uncertain origin. The following procedure allows the reader to discern the past, present, and future. Three cups of three various materials are needed.

Old instructions state that the weather must have been calm for three days prior to the divination, and that the diviner be dressed in white. Fill a silver cup with wine, a copper cup with oil, and a vessel of glass with water. Scry in the silver cup to view the past, in the copper cup to see present events, and in the glass to discover the future. Use of these three scrying tools is ideal when the past, present, and future all pertain to the question—which is usually the case.

Gold cups filled with water were also sometimes used for gazing, but these have always been out of the reach of most diviners. A variant of this practice consists of placing a gold ring in a glass of water. Set this glass before a mirror and gaze into the ring's reflection in the looking glass.

Natural bodies of water provide excellent gazing tools. A calm lake or a small pool that is continuously filled by a running stream is ideal. Sit before the lake or pool. Shut out all distractions and gaze into the water. If appropriate, ask a question. You will see what you need to know.

Finally, toss a lump of gold into a well. The water will become clearer and, thus, more conducive to scrying. (Silver was probably more often used in this rite than gold. This is a relic of the days in which wells were considered to be sacred and the gold or silver was an offering to the well's spirit or attendant deity.)

Other methods of water gazing include watching the waves at a beach, gazing into the sea from a high point that juts into it, scrying in the reflections of the sun sent up by water against a flat surface, and many other techniques.

Other Forms of Water Divination

Floating

In addition to scrying, water has been used in a number of ways to determine the future. One of these has been in use since ancient Greek times. Take a specific object (a slice of bread, a leaf, or some other light object) to a lake or spring. While asking a yes or no question, throw the object into the water. If it sinks, the answer is yes; if it continues to float, or sinks but rises and is washed up on the bank, no.

To determine the faithfulness of a lover, toss a scarf onto the surface of a pond or lake. If the scarf floats to the north, she or he has been faithful. If to the south there is doubt in this regard.

A charming form of divination with water has been used the world over. It's a variation of the one performed with the lake described above. Place a small flower in the bottom of a large bowl. Asking your question, pour water into the bowl. If the flower floats after a few moments, the answer is yes. If it remains at the bottom of the bowl, the answer is no. If it rises but then sinks, no answer is possible at this time. (Similar techniques were used in places as distant in time and space as ancient Hawaii and Greece.)

A similar divination requires nothing more than three pieces of paper, a large bowl, and water. Write "yes" on one piece of paper, "no" on the second, and leave the third blank. Place them into the bowl. Ask your question and pour water into the bowl. The first that rises to the surface of the water answers your question. If this is the blank paper, it indicates that no answer can be produced at this time.

To discover the state of the weather at sea, throw a piece of bread into a well. If it floats, all will be calm. However, if it sinks, foul weather is predicted; don't unfurl the sails that day.

Wells and Ponds

Wells are potent divinatory tools. To find the answer to any binary question, toss a stone into a well. The number of bubbles that rise from the stone's journey to the bottom reveal the response: an odd number signifies no, while an even number of bubbles is a yes.

The act of throwing a coin into a well is still in common use, and stems from the ancient practice of tossing heavy objects into still bodies of water and judging the future by the number of rings so created. At times, stones of specific shapes were used: one square, one triangular, and one round stone were recommended. Throw these three, or just one stone, into the water. Watch the undulations created on the water's surface.

Wells are also used in a curious form of scrying. Go to a working, operational well alone at dusk or dawn. Gaze into the water. If you see a symbol, remember it. After it has disappeared, toss a rock into the well. If you can hear an echo of the rock's splash, the message is true.

An unusual form of water divination requires very specific conditions but is well worth the time and wait involved. It can be performed only at night. You'll need to find a shallow, artificial pool (I use the pool below a fountain after it's been turned off for the evening). The water in this pool must be still. A light should shine nearby onto the water. Wait until it begins to rain. A gentle rain, one with widely interspersed drops, is absolutely necessary. Sit or stand beside the fountain and ask a question. If the light is bright enough, it will illuminate the rain drops falling onto the water. Each drop will send a single ring radiating outward as it hits. Watch the size of these rings. If most are small and last less than a second, the answer is yes. If most are large and last for a longer time, the answer is no.

Listening to Water

Yet another method of consulting the water oracle consists of sitting or lying beside a stream or river running over rocks. Still your mind and listen to the murmuring of the water. A picture may form in your mind in response to your question.

Goldfish

An apparently modern form of water divination uses a fish bowl and goldfish. Place the bowl on a table. Position a bright light so that it shines through the bowl onto the wall above and behind it (block the light so that its beam is narrow; a flashlight may prove effective). As the light shines through the bowl, the fishes' movements will create shadows on the wall that may reveal the future.

Steam

Steam can also provide divinatory responses. This requires a mirror hung on a wall and a low table placed before it. Fill a large pot with water and heat the water to boiling on the stove. Remove the pot and place it on a hot pad before the mirror. As the steam rises, it will cloud the mirror. You may gaze in the misty mirror, or wait for the steam to condense and drip down its silvered face. The drips may form themselves into a letter or letters, which can be then interpreted.

9

Fire, Candles, Smoke, and Ash

The use of fire to determine the future is known as *pyromancy*. It includes a variety of techniques, many of which are included here, and can provide fascinating insights into our tomorrows.

In many cultures, fire was considered to be a sacred substance. Legends speak of heroic figures stealing fire from the deities and presenting this important gift to their human worshippers. This element was directly linked with the sun and, thus, with the fertility of the earth. Yet it has also always been feared, as uncontrolled fire can produce disaster and death.

Nevertheless, even dreaming of fire is still considered to be an omen of good fortune, happiness, and hope. This is an obvious survival of the ancient respect for this primal element.

Fire's ability to change solid objects into ash that can be blown away in the slightest breeze; its warmth-giving properties and the mysterious nature of its flickering flames have caused it to be a popular tool of divination, but it should be used with care. All the usual safety precautions regarding fire must be followed. Don't light fires in the forest, clear the ground around all outdoor fires, make sure the damper in the chimney is open, and don't leave candles burning unattended for long periods of time. Also ensure that only flame-proof candle holders are used.

Fire

Fire Gazing

This ancient technique can produce surprising results. Sit before a roaring fire. Ask your question and gaze into the flames while the fire burns down. Within the flames, or in the sparkling, glowing coals below them, images of the future may appear. Interpret them with symbolic thought.

It's best to limit gazing time to about five minutes, but there's no need to check your watch. Allow the images to come to you for an appropriate time.

Fire Reading

An alternate version of fire gazing consists of lighting a fire and reading the future according to its appearance. While there are many variants of the signs and their meanings, the following list is considered to be fairly accurate:

- If, after stirring the fire, it burns brightly, a loved one far from home is safe and happy.

- Pale flames foretell the approach of bad weather.

- If the fire suddenly blazes up in a raging inferno, a stranger will soon arrive.

- Blue flames indicate the approach of a storm.

- Showers of sparks from a fire indicate that news of some importance will reach you shortly.

- When the fire seems to be buzzing (as opposed to crackling), storms are at hand.

- Sparks flying from the fire indicate a coming altercation in the household.

- If a fire refuses to light, hard work will be required in the future.

- If the fire lights quickly, visitors are to be expected.

- A very bright fire is a sign of rain.

- A sputtering fire betokens snow.

- When the fire talks, trouble is ahead. You may see other signs; interpret them accordingly.

Heat and Straws

Sideromancy is a form of fire divination that utilizes heat and straws. On the stove, heat a skillet with a flat bottom. Carefully turn it over and place it on a heat-proof surface. Scatter several straws (not drinking straws; the stems of grains such as wheat, oats, barley, etc.) onto the skillet's heated bottom. Watch the straws gyrate and dance as they begin to burn and smoke, and discover the future from their actions.

Burnings

Write a question concerning the future on a small piece of paper. Place it face-down on a flat, heat-proof surface.

Light one corner of the paper with a match. If the entire paper burns, the answer is yes. If only part of the paper is destroyed, the answer is no.

Daphnomancy is yet another form of fire divination. It consists of tossing laurel branches or leaves into a fire. To find the answer to a yes or no question, say the following directly to the fire:

> *Fire, fire, blessed fire*
> *Unto fortune I aspire*
> *Now I hope that I may see*
> *The future that will come to me.*

Then state your question while tossing five bay leaves onto the fire, or onto its coals. If they crackle and splutter while burning, the answer is yes. If they burn silently, the answer is no.

Alternately, throw a flammable object into the fire while asking a question. If it doesn't burn or if it burns more slowly than usual, the signs are favorable, or the answer is yes. If it burns, unfavorable or no. This is technically known as *causimomancy*, a branch of pyromancy.

Wooden matches also play a role in fire divination. Ask a yes or no question. Light a match and hold it straight up. If the head curves toward the left while burning, the answer is no. If to the right, yes.

Candles

The observation of the burning of candles is a time-honored art. It shares with oil-lamp divination the term *lychnomancy*. Indeed, oil lamps are the ancient forerunners of candles as we know them today. It also seems to be a modern version of the classical practice of *lampadomancy*, in which the flames of torches were observed for omens of the future. (See Appendix 1: A Dictionary of Divinations.)

A curious candle divination was once used to discover the presence of treasure within a cave. A lantern and a beeswax candle were taken into the cave. The candle was attached to a hazel branch that naturally formed a "w." The candle was lit and the diviner walked deeper into the cave. If the candle sparked, treasure lay nearby. If it burned normally, no treasure was present. When the diviner reached the treasure's specific location, the candle's flame would flare up, emit a tremendous number of sparks, and would then suddenly go out. (This is why the lantern was also brought, to provide illumination.) It is doubtful that such techniques are in use today, but this is an excellent example of one of the numerous ways that humans have relied on candles to discover the unknown.

To perform any of the following rites, choose a room not usually subject to winds or drafts. Night is the preferred time, and it's best to lower the lights. Use white candles, except where otherwise indicated.

Light a candle and place it in its holder. Sit or stand before it and search for signs from the flame itself and its wick. If the candle refuses to light, a storm is probably on the way. If the flame seems dim, it may be best to hold off on plans for the time being. An extremely bright flame is a sign of good fortune, but if it quickly grows smaller, the luck will be temporary.

If the flame waves about, some other form of bad weather may be coming, or a great change in circumstances is foretold. A spark visible in the wick indicates the imminent arrival of good news. If the flame turns in a circle or seems to form a spiral, danger is forecast. Finally, a halo around the flame indicates an approaching storm.

Another method of reading candles involves watching the manner in which the molten wax drips down the candle's sides. Though white candles can be used for this purpose, you may wish to choose one whose color matches the nature of your question, as listed below:

White: All questions.

Purple: Position, authority.

Blue: Sickness, health, and recovery.

Green: Family, children, births, money, jobs.

Yellow: Relocation for work, moving in general, passing tests, communication (upcoming meetings, letters, phone calls), theories.

Orange: Physical actions and activity of all kinds.

Red: Love, relationships.

Pink: Friendships.

Place the candle in a holder. Ask a yes or no question while lighting its wick. Watch it for some time. If wax drips only on the left side, the answer is no. If on the right, yes. If equally on both sides, no response is possible. If no wax drips down, ask again later.

An exceedingly easy way to find an answer to a question: obtain two small candles, such as those placed on birthday cakes. Choose their colors according to the above list. Place these candles in their holders and stick them into a block of clay, a piece of foam, or a potato, cut in half, laid cut-side down.

With two matches, simultaneously light the candles. Settle before them while asking your, question. The first to burn out reveals the answer: the left one, no; the right one, yes. (These candles burn out quite rapidly.)

Alternately, light a candle, ask a question, and observe the flame's motion. If the flame or the wick bends toward you, the answer is yes. If it bends away from you, no.

A technique geared to predicting the future happiness or otherwise for those living in the same house can also be used. This divination is traditionally performed on either Halloween or New Year's Eve, with the purpose of revealing fortunes for the coming twelve months.

Place two candles in holders on the mantle above the fireplace (or on the kitchen table, if there is no fireplace). Light the candle wicks and watch the flames' movements.

If the candles burn well with bright, long flames, good fortune for the household is predicted. If the flames are short, dim, spluttering, or if they send up clouds of smoke, troubles will have to be faced. If, on the other hand, they seem to burn in a normal manner, so, too, will life continue on its present course for those who live in the house.

To determine the character of the coming year, wait until Halloween or New Year's Eve. On that night, light a candle and go outside. Walk around your house clockwise and return inside. If you can accomplish this without the flame being extinguished the coming year will be most fortunate.

A rather unusual form of candle divination involves the remarkable properties of fresh lemon juice. Obtain a clean ink pen (not a ballpoint or felt-tip, but the type once in common use in which the writing tip was dipped into a bottle of ink). Since neither an ink-filled pen nor a pencil can be used, a sharpened, short stick may be substituted.

Squeeze the juice from one lemon into a small bowl. Lay three, five, or seven pieces of paper on a flat surface. Dipping the pen into the lemon juice, write a possible future on each piece of paper with the juice; the juice here acts as the ink. Since lemon juice is invisible, and difficult to write with, reduce these futures to just a few words. Allow them to thoroughly dry.

Light a candle. Place the slips of paper in a bowl. Mix them thoroughly with your left hand, then choose one at random. Hold the chosen paper close enough to the flame to heat it but not to burn it. The heat will reveal the future written on the paper as the lemon juice darkens. This will determine the possible future.

Smoke

Libanomancy (also known as *capnomancy* and *thurifumia*) consists of the observation of smoke as it rises from a fire, from burning objects, or from incense. The Babylonians performed it, as did the Greeks, who carefully watched the smoke rising from the burning food offered in sacrifice to their deities. Many cultures have practiced similar rites. The Semang of Malaysia, a nomadic people, would light a fire before setting up camp each night. If the smoke rose straight up, the location was safe. If it wafted into the jungle, there was danger of attacks by tigers. Another site was chosen.

Though these are quite ancient techniques, modern forms are still in use. One of these is termed "smoke reading." Light a candle. Pass a plain white card through the flame three times while asking a question. (Do this quickly to avoid setting the card on fire). Interpret the resulting carbon deposits left on the underside of the card with symbolic thought. This may require a bit of work.

There are many older techniques. Build a fire outside in a safe place while asking a yes/no question. Watch the smoke. If it rises straight and lightly into the air, a positive answer has been received. If, however, it hangs heavily around the fire, the reverse is true.

The second method of capnomancy involves burning specific objects and observing the smoke that rises from them. Asking your question, throw a handful of poppy seeds onto the burning coals of a dying fire. The responses are read in the same manner described in the paragraph above.

Alternately, throw a handful of cedar shavings (available in almost all pet supply stores and many supermarkets) onto the coals while asking your question and, once again, read the omens according to the first method described above. This is of Babylonian origin.

An easier technique requires nothing more exotic than burning an incense stick. Though any type can be used, sandalwood seems to produce the best results. Hold the incense stick between your hands and ask your question. Light it, set it in its holder, and gaze into the smoke. A message may be revealed to you by the smoke's appearance or actions. (See the foregoing for specific omens from the rising smoke.)

Finally, watch the smoke rising from extinguished candles. If it moves to the right, the answer is yes. If to the left, no.

Ashes

Divination from ashes is a logical development from the other forms described above. Ashes, the product of fire's transformative properties, were once highly respected. They can still be used to determine the future.

Collect ashes from dead fires or the fireplace. Outside, in a place where the wind usually blows at some time, scatter the ashes to a good depth in a rectangular shape on the ground. While asking your question regarding the future, use a finger to write the word "yes" in the ashes to the right and "no" to the left. Leave them undisturbed overnight.

In the morning, study the ashes. If both words are clearly legible, no answer is possible at this time. If one has been obliterated by animal tracks, the wind, or by some other force, the remaining word ("yes" or "no") reveals the answer to your question. If both words are gone, again, no answer has been given.

Alternately, write in the ashes two or three words that encapsulate your question, such as "Move next month." The next morning you'll probably find that some of the letters have been destroyed. Piece together the remaining letters to reveal the future.

10

Wind, Clouds, and Birds

*A*eromancy (divination by the observation of provoked omens involving atmospheric phenomena, including the wind and the appearance of clouds) is a timeless practice. The sky provides a huge arena in which a number of various signs may occur, and has long been relied upon as an accurate tool for predicting the future.

Birds may also be included under this heading, as they move across the sky and greatly rely on the winds to support them for long-distance travel. This chapter details two forms of aeromancy as well as the old techniques of watching for omens derived from birds.

Wind

Divination from observation of the winds is an ancient practice. A form of aeromancy, it was specifically known as *austromancy*.

Wind has always been a mysterious phenomena. For countless centuries, humans had no understanding of the forces that create breezes, gusts, whirlwinds, and storms. Many believed that wind was actually the breath of their deities; alternately, some thought that specific types of winds, particularly hot winds, were the work of demons.

Several techniques involving wind can be used. Most of the ancient forms were created and used in limited geographical locations, where winds stemming from certain directions were known to predict events. Much of this information has been lost. However, general forms of wind divination are also available for use.

Go to a place where few trees or buildings block the wind. If it's already windy, wait until the air grows calm. Ask a yes or no question and watch the winds.

If, on rising, the winds blow to the north, the answer is favorable; to the east, unfavorable; to the south, unfavorable; to the west, favorable (you may need to bring along a compass). If no wind rises within nine minutes, no response is immediately possible.

If, in the unlikely event that a whirlwind—sometimes known as a "dust devil"—suddenly appears, it is an unfavorable omen. Further divinations using other techniques may be necessary to determine the exact nature of such a warning.

Another method uses the winds in a different manner. Write five possible futures, or five choices that you're currently facing, on five round pieces of paper. Take these outside to a windy place. Draw a circle on the ground and lay the papers within it. The wind will eventually rise and blow the papers from the circle.

The last paper to remain within the circle reveals the best possible choice (or the most likely future event). If they're all simultaneously removed by the wind from the circle, no response is possible at this time. If no wind rises, again, there is no answer. (Please don't litter—gather the papers after use and dispose of them properly.)

The wind has also been used in a number of other ingenious ways. For example, sit beside a lake (or even a swimming pool). Ask a question and watch the water's surface. If the wind picks up and produces ripples on the water's surface, the answer is yes. If not, no.

Clouds

On a bright windy day, clouds often pass overhead in fantastic shapes. We usually take them for granted or are unaware of their presence, but occasionally we'll be struck by the appearance of a cloud and may well wonder why we ever stopped looking at them.

Watching the clouds for answers to questions is a delightful and possibly illuminating practice. It's also quite relaxing and enjoyable. Cloud watching is directly related to other gazing techniques. It may require symbolic thought to fully penetrate the inner meaning of the presented response.

On a day when clouds race across the sky, or when thunderheads build up to impressive size, sit or stand with your back to the sun and look up toward the sky. (Ideally, it shouldn't be completely overcast.) Think of your question and gaze into the clouds.

Study their shapes, blinking normally. Soon they may form a symbol, or you may become aware of a symbol that was already present. Examine this image and determine what connection it has with your question. This art doesn't always require interpretation—if the diviner earnestly seeks messages from the clouds, they may plainly reveal the future in recognizable shapes.

Birds

Known as *ornithomancy*, the observation of birds is a form of provoked omen-reading. Birds have long been thought to possess special abilities to communicate the future, perhaps because they're one of the few creatures that possess the ability to fly.

Birds were considered to be messengers of the goddesses and gods. This seemed perfectly natural, as birds could fly directly to them at any time. Possessed of all wisdom from these interactions with deity, birds were favored tools of divination in most cultures. Scholars suggest that this usage stemmed from the practice of sailors who, while lost at sea, followed flocks of birds back to shore.

Omens are taken from their sudden appearance; the direction in which they fly; their cries; their number; the manner in which they settle on the ground and their movements thereafter. A specialized ancient form of bird divination consisted of releasing a captive bird and determining the future according to the direction of its flight.

Some ancient cultures preferred specific types of birds, and most of these were predatory. The Greeks and Romans looked to eagles, ravens, carrion crows, and vultures, while the ancient Germans also favored the first three of this short list. Celtic priestesses and priests turned to crows, eagles, and wrens. Many heroic figures from these ancient culture were described as possessing the ability to under-stand the language of birds and to converse with them. This may be a veiled reference to the ability to practice or-nithomancy.

The Romans brought the technique of bird divination to a high science. Their augurs followed specific procedures. The bird diviner sat in a tent situated on a hill. Wearing a special robe, he described an area in the visible sky with an augural staff; within these bounds the omens were to occur. After pouring out libations of wine, a prayer was uttered beseeching the god Jupiter to "grant that there be unerring signs within the boundaries that I have described." Accord-ing to the appearance of birds and their behavior, the augur stated that "the birds approve" or "the birds disapprove."

Bird divination was in use throughout the world. The ancient Aztecs wandered about, aimlessly searching for a proper place to build their magnificent new city. They searched for signs on a daily basis. Finally, they saw an eagle sitting on a cactus with a snake in its mouth. This was obviously an omen of the highest order, and it directly led to the foundation of what is now known as Mexico City. The image of this omen appears to this day on the colorful Mexican flag.

By the 1800s, the once noble art of ornithomancy had been reduced in Italy to the activities of street fortune-tell-ers, who kept trained parakeets. Those who wished to have their fortunes told would seek out such a soothsayer and pay a small sum. The parakeet would choose at random a slip of paper on which the person's fortune was revealed.

Some birds are still linked with divinatory messages. In the United States, for example, the red bird is a prognosticator. If you see one, make a wish. If the bird flies upward or to the east, the wish will come true.

Recent studies have shown that birds are rapidly disappearing due to loss of habitat and the continuing use of pesticides. Steps are being taken to ensure their continued survival, and some species are beginning to return in greater numbers. Still, many birds are on the brink of extinction. In Hawaii, the songs of dozens of types of birds that once lived nowhere else but on those islands have been silenced. Many organizations are fortunately directly involved in the preservation of wild birds.

Bird divination is an enjoyable way of determining the future. Go to a place with many trees and a source of water and food for the birds. Stand or sit and ask your question. Turn your face toward the sky and watch for birds.

If birds suddenly fly across the sky from the left to the right, the answer is favorable. If from the right to the left, unfavorable. If no birds appear, ask again later.

If birds fly directly toward and over you, the signs are favorable, or the answer is yes. If directly overhead and away from you, unfavorable or no.

Here are some other factors to keep in mind when practicing bird divination:

1. Some birds are thought to be fortunate, others unfortunate (see the list that follows). To see a fortunate bird on the left greatly diminishes its positive aspects; an unfortunate bird on the right will bring a small degree of bad luck. However, fortunate birds on the

right and unfortunate birds on the left are clear signs and need little interpretation. This information, however, can be ignored if desired.

2. The number of birds pursuing the same path or perching on the same object during your observation also determines the answer: an even number is positive; an odd number is negative. Four birds flying from the left to the right is considered to be the most auspicious sign. Three birds flying from the left to the right is unfavorable. Thus, their number may also be taken into consideration. Once again, if an odd number of birds fly in the positive direction, ascertain their message as best as you can. ("Favorable" here may indicate a positive divinatory response to a yes or no question; "unfavorable"' as a negative response.)

3. The cries of birds, when heard during divination, can also be of divinatory use. One or two calls are positive; three, negative. A greater number of cries indicates that the birds aren't immediately available for answers.

4. The height at which birds fly plays its role in this form of divination. Birds of good omen flying high foretell extremely good luck; lower, a lessened positive event. Similarly, unfortunate birds flying at high altitudes are extremely ill-omened; less so at lower elevations.

5. When you begin to work with the birds of your area (and they needn't be the predatory type, though hawks and eagles are ideal) you may find that a particular species seems to give the best results. If so,

it's safe to ignore omens from other types of birds and rely on this species for messages.

Another type of bird divination relies on the appearance of specific types of birds during a session. The following list has been largely gathered from European and American sources, but could easily be expanded a hundredfold. Note: fortunate birds indicate positive responses to question; unfortunate birds, negative responses.

Blackbird: A *fortunate* omen whenever seen, especially two blackbirds sitting together.

Bluebird: A *fortunate* symbol of happiness.

Crow: Usually thought of as an *unfortunate* omen, though the number of its cries is considered to be of greater significance. One is favorable, two unfavorable, three favorable.

Dove: Highly *fortunate*. Predicts peace, love, and happiness.

Duck: *Fortunate*. Your relationship will be stable.

Eagle: Often considered to be *unfortunate*, though eagles can also be viewed as symbols of power and strength. Sighting one may indicate that you'll rise above current problems and emerge successfully.

Gull: *Fortunate*. You may soon travel. If the trip involves business, it will be financially successful. If a vacation, you'll enjoy yourself.

Heron: *Unfortunate*. Hard times ahead.

Hummingbird: The appearance of these delightful birds is quite *fortunate*, for they betoken love, marriage, or pregnancy.

Lark: Another *fortunate* bird representative of love, the lark can also predict future health or illness. If a sick person watches a lark sitting on a branch she or he can determine the likelihood of recovery. If the lark turns its head from the ill person, the sickness will continue for some time. If, however, it stares directly at the diviner, recovery will soon occur.

Magpie: Both *fortunate* and *unfortunate*. Usually thought to be an omen of disaster, the number of these birds is indicative of a wide range of predictions. One, misfortune. Two, happiness (and possibly marriage). Three, a delightful trip. Four signifies the arrival of good news, while five indicates that friends will visit. Any number higher than five is considered to be unfavorable.

Oriole: *Fortunate*. Happiness and peace are in the future.

Owl: Usually considered to be *unfortunate*, for in most countries owls are seen as omens of death or disaster, one ancient divinatory meaning for this bird's appearance was quite different: wisdom would be bestowed upon the observer.

Quail: A peaceful household is predicted by the appearance of a quail. A *fortunate* bird. If arguments are raging, they'll soon end.

Raven: Despite its sleek black appearance, the raven can be a positive omen, depending on the number seen. One raven betokens sadness; two, happiness; three, marriage; four, birth. Ravens are considered by some cultures to be the most prophetic of all birds. Both *fortunate* and *unfortunate.*

Robin: *Fortunate.* The appearance of a robin portends a harmonious home life.

Sparrow: This homely little bird, when it appears during divination, ensures domestic tranquility. Quite *fortunate.*

Swallow: A *fortunate sign,* whether perching or flying to the right. Joy is in the future.

Stork: Fairly *fortunate.* The future will largely be positive; children may be involved.

Swallow: *Fortunate.* Love and luck.

Wren: A *fortunate* sign concerning the future. Wrens are the luckiest of all birds.

11

Plants and Herbs

Plants have long been called upon to provide glimpses of the future. This form of divination, termed botanomancy, uses plants in innumerable ways: they're placed beneath the pillow to create prophetic dreams; are sown and observed as they grow; are used as pendulums; and are tossed into water, air, or fire. Plants seen unexpectedly are responsible for a wide range of omens, especially those relating to the weather. Some plants have quite curious uses.

The rationale for the use of plants in divination is clear: they are (or were) living things, they have closer ties to human life than most other tools of prognostication; thus, they may possess the ability to more accurately predict our lives. Additionally, certain types of plants have long been recognized as possessing specific nonphysical energies, and some forms of divination capitalize upon this phenomenon. I hasten to add, however, that belief in such energies isn't necessary to the practice of botanomancy. The following techniques are within the realm of divination, not magic.

For centuries, cultures in all parts of the world relied on hallucinogenic, narcotic, or poisonous plants to produce visions or to in some other way assist divinatory rites. Peyote use among the Huichols of central Mexico is perhaps one of the most famous examples. The peoples of North, Central, and South America also relied on hallucinogenic plants to obtain answers to questions.

Drug use of this kind is sometimes classified as divination but, in all save a few isolated peoples, this practice as a socially accepted form of prognostication has fortunately died out. Such rites are dangerous, for the diviner has no control over the operation once she or he is under the influence. Additionally, much delusion occurs while the body and brain are within the drug's grip.

No information of value concerning the present or future can be gained by the ritual use of drugs; thus, none of these plants will be discussed here.

I've included here several methods of using plants to assist in discovering the future. Other methods of divination with plants will be found in Chapter 8: Water; Chapter 9: Fire, Candles, Smoke, and Ash; and Chapter 14: In Matters of Love.

A General Plant Divination

Fill five flower pots with the same kind of dirt. Plant in each pot a seed of the same type of flower, on the same day and at the same time. Ensure that they have the same exposure to sunlight (if applicable). For best results, do this on the day of the full moon.

On a small piece of tape, write an expected or hoped-for future and apply this to the side of one pot. Continue until all five pots have been designated with five different futures. (Small signs attached to sticks or twigs may also be used, thrust into the earth near the pot's side.) Water as usual. The seed that first germinates determines the event that will most likely occur in the near future.

The Apple

Using a silver knife, peel an apple so that it comes off the fruit in one unbroken strip. (If the peel breaks while paring, try again at a later time—and eat the apple.)

When you've been successful, ask your question and throw the peel over your left shoulder. It will produce a shape on the floor behind you. If this shape is anything other than an "O" or "U", the answer is yes.

Another apple divination is related to the daisy rite described below. It exists in many variants; here's one of the most popular. Find an apple that still has its stem end attached. Ask your question. Hold the apple in your left hand and, with your right, begin twisting the stem. With each twist, say "yes" or "no." The word that you say when the stem twists off (or directly prior to this occurrence) signifies the answer to your question.

The Daisy

This is perhaps the best-known of all plant divinations. As you probably know, it consists of removing each petal from the daisy while saying "She loves me, she loves me not." (The masculine pronoun is used where appropriate.) The word stated as the last petal is removed reveals the truth. Any daisy-like flower can be used for this technique.

A second form of daisy divination isn't limited to matters of love. Ask a binary question. As you pluck each petal, say "yes" or "no." As the last petal falls, the answer has been given.

This type of procedure represents a genuine form of divination, proven effective during many centuries of practice. However, few persons today (especially the children who constitute its usual practitioners) are probably aware of this technique's great antiquity.

The Dandelion

To discover whether a wish will come true, and how soon, find a dandelion that has gone to seed. Ask whether some desired wish will come true. Blow hard against the seeds. If all the seeds fly off, your wish will be shortly granted. If a few seeds remain, a bit of time will be necessary for this to occur. If many seeds are left, your desire will not be granted.

An alternate method consists of thinking of your husband, wife, or mate while blowing on a dandelion. If all the seeds immediately fly away, the relationship is stable. If not, problems may be in the offing.

A third method: blow away the winged seeds. If they immediately fall to the ground, the answer is no. If they float away on the wind, yes.

Leaves

Sycomancy (divination with leaves) was once practiced solely with the leaves of fig trees. However, today it can be used with the leaves of any type of tree provided that they're large enough for our purposes.

Find a suitable leaf. Write a question upon the leaf. Place it in a safe spot. If it quickly withers and dries, the prospects aren't rosy. However, if it remains fresh and dries slowly, the signs are favorable.

A related practice consists of lying beneath the tree and listening to the sound of the wind moving through the leaves to produce prophecies.

Alternately, sit beneath a large, leafy tree when the sun is shining, the sky is clear, and a breeze freshens the air. Face west to discover the past; north the present, and east the future. Ask your question. Watch the shadows created by the sun shining through the moving leaves. Look for symbols and interpret them in accordance with your query.

Leaves are used in other ways. To know if the coming year will be happy or sad, go to a tree in autumn as it is loosening its leaves. Every leaf that you catch in mid-air as it falls portends a lucky week. An alternate version is to stand beneath an apple tree in spring and catch the petals of the fragrant blossoms as they fall. Each petal is a sign of a month of good fortune. This is a rather difficult art; the leaves and petals twist and sway in the wind, and some practice may be necessary before successful results can be achieved.

Onion

Cromniomancy is a technique that uses onions. It's quite simple to perform, though it takes several weeks to discover the response. Obtain three fresh round onions. Place them in a spot where they can remain undisturbed for some time. Name the left onion "yes," the middle onion "maybe," and the right onion "no." The first onion to sprout determines the answer to your question. If the onion's sprout points toward you, the accuracy of the response is strengthened.

Rose

Three methods of divination utilizing roses are available for use. The first, known as *phyllorhodomancy*, consists of placing a fresh rose petal in the palm of your left hand, then smartly snapping your right hand against the petal. If this creates a loud sound, the signs are favorable or the answer is yes. If there is little sound, the reverse has been divined. (This practice is of ancient Greek origin.)

Alternately, obtain three fresh roses. Place these in three vases that aren't filled with water. Name the left rose "yes," the middle rose "no answer" and the right rose "no." The flower that remains fresh after the other two have withered reveals the outcome. Check them several times a day to observe their progress.

Finally, a rose love oracle: fill a basin with rose water (or, failing this rather expensive commodity, plain water). Pluck three leaves from a rose plant. Name each for a specific person that you wish to become involved with (but are having difficulty making up your mind). Place these on the surface of the rose water. The leaf that floats for the longest time on the water's surface indicates the favored choice.

Plant Omens

Observing plants for omens of the future is becoming increasingly difficult. No longer do meadows or prairies lie just beyond the village. Parks are usually planted and maintained, and wild plants are scrupulously removed. Some plants manage to raise their heads between the cracks of broken concrete, but few are hardy enough to survive these harsh growing conditions.

It was far different in the past. Most travel was done on foot or horseback. For amusement, enlightenment, and simply to pass the time, travelers would watch the natural world around them. One of the wonders that they would search for was the sudden and unexpected appearance of plants. Generally speaking, the first plant of a specific kind that's seen in the spring was considered a prediction of good fortune.

Just a few specific plants and their divinatory meanings are listed below:

Aloe: To see this common plant in bloom (a rare occurrence) is an omen of fortune.

Daffodil: Though it's considered unlucky to see the first daffodil in spring, the observer will, somewhat curiously, earn "more gold than silver" in the coming year.

Fir: Seeing a fir tree in an unusual locale is a sign of future mischief and challenges.

Four-Leaf Clover: The nearly universal sign of good luck.

Hay: Seeing a load of fresh hay is a positive sign.

Holly: Good luck.

Laurel: Peace and goodwill.

Lilac: Finding a rare five-petaled lilac is an omen of great luck. This is highly unusual, but it does occur.

Lily: Celibacy.

Mistletoe: Mysteries.

Myrtle: Seen flowering, a sign of good fortune.

Nettle: Challenges ahead.

Poppy: An ill omen.

Rose: Seeing the flower is an omen of love.

Wisteria: In bloom, seen unexpectedly, this is an omen that your love is faithful, or that she or he is thinking about you at that moment.

12

The Casting of Lots

The casting of lots (also known as *sortilege*), one of the oldest forms of divination, was in use in ancient Babylon, Greece, Rome, Germany, and elsewhere. Even the Chinese art of casting yarrow stalks to consult the I Ching is a related method. In Africa and Oceania, this technique consists of the tossing of shells and other objects which, when studied according to a set of traditional interpretations, reveal the future. This last practice is still in use, as are related systems found among some African countries that utilize bones and other similar objects. In West Africa, for example, the Dahomeans pray to the goddess Fa, then toss betel nuts onto the ground. From their relative positions they divine the future.

The still popular method of drawing straws to select an individual for a specific task is a related practice. The English phrase "my lot in life" and the concept of the lottery (now held to determine winners of cash) are derived from the practice as well. A California voter's pamphlet prepared by the Registrar of Voters offers information concerning the political parties listed in the order dictated by lot.

Perhaps the commonest form of lot casting in use today is the flipping of a coin to determine a victor in an altercation. Though this may seem to be a modern practice, it actually dates to ancient Rome. During Julius Caesar's reign, most coins bore a likeness of his face on one side. When a disagreement arose, a coin was flipped to allow the god (that is, Caesar) to determine the winner. If the coin landed face-up, the one who had called heads was the winner, for Caesar had appeared.

Anciently, the casting of lots seems to have been created for the express purpose of selecting a person suitable for a particular social role—that is, to determine the will of the deities. In this sense it was somewhat akin to an election, although only the deities voted. However, it seems that lots were also used to gain insight and guidance concerning a wide variety of areas of human life.

The forms of lot casting described in this chapter include the use of dice (*cleromancy*), stones (*pessomancy*), and staves or sticks. It is quite easy to create your own forms. Simply apply the same principles and techniques with new tools.

Modern forms of this type of divination include the ever popular casting of stones or staves upon which runes have been painted or carved. Reliable guides to this practice can be found in the bibliography.

Cleromancy

Dice were perhaps one of the first tools used in lot casting. The earliest types of dice were made from the knucklebones of certain types of animals. These afforded sides upon which numbers or other symbols could be written, and could readily be cast to provide a reading. Perhaps not much later, humans discovered that dice could also be produced with clay. This provided smoother surfaces on which to write or carve. Clay dice were the forerunners of the plastic form in use today.

Though the practice itself is ancient, most forms of dice divination still in use seem to have been established in the late nineteenth and early twentieth centuries. These modern versions were created for amusement. Fortunetelling pamphlets and books of the era usually included directions for the use of dice in divination. Though rarely employed today, this simple system can provide a quick insight into the future.

The message received is said to usually come true within nine days. For some curious reason, attempting dice divination is not recommended on Monday or Wednesday.

Dice divination requires three dice. This practice is somewhat limited, as the oracle itself determines the message (that is, it won't answer a specific question). Use your insight to broaden the dice's prognostications.

To proceed, place three dice of the same size either into a cup or between your hands. Shake them vigorously and allow them to fall onto a piece of velvet. Add the numbers that appear on the upper surfaces of the dice, then determine your fortune according to this list:

Three: The smallest number that can appear. Pleasant surprises in the very near future.

Four: Unpleasantness of some kind may occur.

Five: Plans will come to fruition; a wish will be granted.

Six: A loss of some kind is forecast.

Seven: Possible difficulties in business, money troubles, gossip and so on.

Eight: Expect criticism.

Nine: Marriage; unions.

Ten: Birth, either of a child or of a new project.

Eleven: A parting, which may be temporary.

Twelve: A message of importance will soon arrive.

Thirteen: Sorrow.

Fourteen: Friendship; help from a new friend.

Fifteen: Begin no new projects for a few days.

Sixteen: A pleasant journey.

Seventeen: A change in plans may soon be necessary.

Eighteen: Success; a wish will be obtained; the very best number to appear. A similar, even more modern version uses dominoes in much the same manner. Different futures are determined by the combination of numbers that appear on a domino selected at random from a pile.

Stones

Another form of lot casting involves the use of small stones (known as *pessomancy*). Gather thirteen white and thirteen black stones. (If you can only find white or light-colored stones, paint thirteen of them black.) All should be of approximately the same size.

While asking your yes/no question, place the stones in a small cloth bag or a metal bowl. Shake the stones. Repeat, then state the question a second and third time.

Reach into the bowl or bag and, with your eyes closed, grab a handful of stones. Remove them and place them on the surface of the table or the ground.

Count the number of each color of stones. If there are more white stones than black, the answer to your question is favorable. If more black stones have been collected, the answer is no. If you've retrieved an equal number of black and white stones, there is no answer at this time. You will need to try again later. (A related practice was in use in old Hawaii, and the Incas used piles of dried corn kernels for a similar purpose.)

A modern form of stone divination apparently originated in Europe. Obtain thirteen stones of uniform size. Using white paint, mark each with one of the following words, on one side only (abbreviate if necessary):

Sun

Moon

Mercury

Venus

Mars

Jupiter

Saturn

Home

Love

Money

News

Travel

Health

The first seven of these are, obviously, the planets together with the sun and moon. The last six represent various aspects of life.

To use the stones, draw a circle one foot in diameter. Shake the stones in a bag and throw them over the circle. Those that fall outside of the circle aren't read. Neither are those that land blank-side-up. Only those stones that are within the circle face-up are consulted.

Here's a list of the stones and their divinatory meanings:

Sun: Great activity; illumination.

Moon: Dreams, fantasies, changeability, the future in motion, healing, secrets.

Mercury: Thought is required.

Venus: Love, beauty, compassion.

Mars: Fights, danger, arguments, altercations, energy.

Jupiter: Money, employment, business.

Saturn: Old age, sustainment, possible health problems.

Home: Family relations, the structure itself.

Love: Relationships, marriage, companionship, separation or divorce (if near Mars or Saturn).

Money: Employment, raises, bills, business, security.

News: Messages of all kinds, letters, faxes.

Travel: Short trips, long trips, business trips, relocation of the home.

Health: Matters of healing and sickness.

Stones that are close to each other are read together. For example, if love appears beside news, you'll receive a message from or about a relationship. If near the Sun, all will become clear concerning your relationship in the future. Near the Moon, your love is mostly a fantasy. If near Mercury, reexamine your relationship. Close to Venus, you are greatly loved. If near Mars, be prepared for a confrontation with your love. Near Jupiter, you've been placing too much importance (love) on money. Near Saturn, the relationship may end soon. Alternately, it may last well into the future.

Other nearby stones can provide additional insight into the situation. If Jupiter appears beside money, look to the next closest stone to determine the nature of the response. If it's news, you may receive a message concerning money, a bill, or even a check.

This system of lot casting can create surprising results if the stones are read with thought and intelligence.

Wooden Lots

A third method is quite simple. Obtain two branches that are as straight as possible (preferably from a tree that has already been cut down). Remove all extraneous twigs, then peel off the bark on one side only of each wooden stick.

Holding the branches, ask your question and roll them on the ground. If, when they come to a complete stop, the two peeled sides are face-up, the answer is yes. If the two unpeeled sides, no. If one of each appears, no reply is possible at this time.

A modern version of this art uses small, square pieces of wood, each of which is marked on one side with the letters of the alphabet (such as the tiles that come with the popular game Scrabble). Place the tiles (there can be more than one for each letter) into a bowl or urn. Shake them while asking your question, or clear your mind.

Pour out the tiles onto a flat surface. Gather those that have landed face-up and set aside those that are blank. With these letters, spell out words that may reveal your future. The first word that you thus spell (unless it's a common word such as "and") will usually pertain to your question. Further words created from the tiles may clarify the response.

13

Crystal Gazing

C rystal gazing (*crystallomancy*) constitutes the ancient art of peering into a crystal ball to receive visions of the past, present, or future. Many cultures, both east and west, have painstakingly fashioned spheres from genuine quartz crystal specifically for this purpose. Crystallomancy's relation to water gazing is obvious and, in fact, quartz crystal was once thought to be water that had been permanently frozen. The coolness of genuine crystal, as well as its clarity, probably gave rise to this belief.

Crystallomancy developed from the common ancient practice of gazing at reflective surfaces (such as fingernails and knife blades), into water (see Chapter 8), into pools of black ink poured into the hand, fires (Chapter 9), and other related practices. These all have a distinct advantage over crystal gazing: they don't require a costly tool. Still, when quartz crystal spheres became available to a greater extent in Europe during the fourteenth century, the wealthy certainly used them or hired others to do so.

A few crystals seem to have been in use at a much earlier date. Almost certainly the Romans introduced crystal gazing throughout Europe. Records indicate that small (one-half inch) spheres of beryl were in common use in Ireland as early as the fifth century. Other stones popular as divining tools include aquamarine, chrysoberyl, and obsidian. These were made into both spheres and square, flat shapes.

There were numerous ways in which the crystal was used. The simplest was to hold it in a darkened room and to gaze into its liquid depths. Alternately, the crystal was taken outside and held up to the sun. The divination then proceeded. (This would almost certainly damage the eyes, and is no longer practiced.)

By the fifteenth century, crystal gazing was an established part of western European ceremonial magic. What was once an elegantly simple art became entangled with Judaeo-Christian mythology. It was transformed into a totally different practice.

In ceremonial magic, magicians were instructed to undergo lengthy purification rituals, recite long invocations, and perform other ritual acts before actually gazing into the crystal. Old instructions directed that the crystal itself be set into a special box or on a stand carved with mystic symbols and sacred names. The crystal was also anointed with olive oil. At times, a prepubescent boy was instructed to gaze into the crystal. The purpose of most of these rituals was to cause a spirit to appear within the crystal.

Fortunately, none of this is necessary, and indeed I know of no one who believes that spirits appear in the crystal. In the hands of a gifted practitioner, images do appear—but these aren't sent by spirits.

Crystallomancy survives today among professional diviners, though most psychics say that they don't actually need the ball to see the future. It's largely present for decorative purposes and to impress the client.

Though crystal gazing is one of the best-known forms of divination, it also happens to be one of the most difficult to master. Additionally, quartz crystal spheres of the appropriate size can be extremely expensive. Still, due to the widespread interest in this art, some instructions are perhaps required here.

Ideally, a crystal sphere is at least two and one-half inches in diameter. It should be cut from quartz crystal, not glass or plastic. The reason usually given for this particular size is that the larger the crystal, the larger the symbols that will be created in it and, thus, the easier it will be to see and interpret them.

The best crystal sphere is perfectly round and clear. Usually, however, most crystal balls of this size contain what are known as veils. Fortunately these in no way hinder the practice of crystallomancy.

As has become common knowledge, quartz crystal is a product of nature possessing a unique set of energies. One of these is its ability to act as a focal point for the seer. The center of the ball seems to draw in the diviner and thus clears the mind of extraneous thoughts.

The purpose of crystal gazing is to produce images within the crystal itself, not in the mind. Some argue that these images actually appear within the gazer's mind, but most practitioners disagree with this statement. While the crystal may, indeed, stimulate psychic awareness, the ball itself creates the images. The awakened psychic awareness is of use simply to assist in the interpretation of the responses received.

This is why crystal gazing requires a seer of a sensitive and receptive nature. Though you needn't be psychic, it helps. Still, most anyone with the willingness to trust the sphere and to be open to its messages will eventually succeed in garnering a symbolic response. Continued practice will only enhance the effectiveness of this technique.

Now to specifics. Crystallomancy is best performed at night, ideally on the full moon or during its waxing. Lower the lights but leave at least one candle or light burning; the room shouldn't be completely dark. Sit with your back to this light source.

The room should be absolutely silent: no crackling fires, no music, no whirling fans; no conversation overheard from another room. Sounds will jeopardize the possibility of seeing anything at all, for they'll distract your mind from the process.

Lay a small piece of black velvet in your left hand. Place the crystal on the black velvet, then cradle it between both your hands. (Alternately, cover a table with black velvet and place the sphere on its stand on the velvet.) Breathe deeply for a few moments to relax your body and mind.

Ask your question. Questions asked of the crystal can concern the past, present, or future. (In fact, during the 1300s crystallomancy was widely used in England to discover thieves and to recover stolen property.)

Gaze into the sphere, not at its outer surface or at any reflections from the room that may be visible. Let yourself go. Blink when necessary—there's no reason to strain your eyes. Also, don't concentrate. This is precisely the opposite state in which you should be. Open your awareness.

The first sign that something is happening will be a clouding of the crystal. It may seem to be filled with a milky-white substance that swirls around within the sphere. Relax and keep gazing. The milkiness may change from white to other colors, but not all seers have experienced this phenomenon. Eventually it will turn black.

Images will then appear within the sphere. Though words are never seen (unless they happen to be written on a piece of paper that's related to your question), the symbols created within the crystal will usually relate to your question. Remember what you see—this is vital for later interpretation. Don't attempt to unlock the message while actually gazing; focus on the symbols themselves.

Eventually, the images will dissolve into the mist, and the mist itself will seem to disappear, as if a curtain had been drawn across the ball. This always marks the end of the gazing session.

Wrap the crystal sphere in the velvet. Place it safely away and immediately interpret the symbols. This can be surprisingly simple if you think in a symbolic manner. For example, if you asked about the future of a loving relationship, and you saw a heart, the message is quite clear (see Chapter 4: Symbolic Thought). If you experience any difficulty in interpretation, write down the symbols seen, in the order in which they were received, and study them at a later time.

Not all crystal responses rely on symbolism. If you've asked to discover the whereabouts of a lost object, you may well see within the crystal the place in which it resides—a drawer, behind the couch, and so on. If several options have been presented to you in some sphere of your life, and you ask which of these is best to take, that option may be clearly expressed.

In the beginning of this work, many find it difficult to move past the point at which the ball appears to cloud over. This may last for weeks. When this happens, wrap the sphere in velvet after an appropriate time and wait at least a day before making the attempt again. Keep practicing on a regular basis. Images will eventually come to you.

A word on leaded glass "crystal" balls. These are less expensive than true quartz crystal. Unfortunately, they lack the unique properties of that stone as well. Still, some have used them to good effect. The balls made from clear plastic aren't recommended; they're easily scratched.

As you continue to work with crystal gazing, you may well discover it to be one of the most evocative and truthful of all forms of divination.

14

In Matters
of Love

In Europe during the eighteenth and nineteenth centuries, many hundreds of divinations were created and used for the sole purpose of determining the diviner's future love life (or the most appropriate mate). These techniques usually employed objects that were available in any home. Many involved plants and some relied on dreams.

Most of these minor arts were used by women. At a time when women weren't encouraged or allowed to go into business, own property, or avoid the duty of raising a family, the future of their emotional lives was of the utmost importance. They had no options: they had to be married and bear children. Thus, the love divinations described here were in frequent use by unmarried young women who wanted to know whom to marry, if the union would be happy, and how many children would be produced.

Though times have changed, fortunately, many unattached women and men still desire an insight into their relationships. It may be a case where assistance is needed to determine the most appropriate mate, when a spouse's fidelity is in question, or to receive signs of what the future will bring if a certain person is married. Because divination can be used for guidance in all aspects of everyday life, it isn't surprising that many techniques are concerned with love.

In Chapter 3, I discussed the inadvisability of performing divination to examine the lives of others. I stated that permission should be granted from the person in question in such cases before the rite. However, some of the techniques described here and elsewhere in this book seem to break this rule. The reason? When we're in a relationship, we give up some control over our lives to our partners, and they to us. Assuming that you act in trust and love, you're truly not snooping and can use these techniques without fear of breaking a divinatory rule. Still, if you're uncomfortable with any such practices, don't use them.

Sometimes communication with our spouses can be difficult. While most of the matters in the methods listed in this chapter might be settled through conversation or deep thought, these rites can be used if your partner is unresponsive. They're also useful if you haven't yet decided on a mate.

This chapter describes only a few of these time-honored rites. I've deliberately omitted those designed to discover the occupation of a young woman's future husband as well as many others that simply don't speak to modern times. Still, the range of divinations included here indicate the astonishing ingenuity of some of these techniques, and are indicative of the enduring importance of love in our lives.

Dreams

This art consists of the production of prophetic dreams through the use of specific tools or actions before bedtime. The most popular means of producing dreams of love is the practice of placing certain objects beneath the pillow. Plants most frequently used for such minor divinations include the four-leaf clover, plantain, yarrow, poplar, mugwort, daisy, and bay. Inquiries regarding the diviner's future love life are stated while falling asleep; the answers are revealed in the dreams that take place that night.

On Midsummer night, collect flowers or small branches from nine different plants (they needn't be those listed above). Place these beneath your pillow and sleep on them. You'll dream of your future love.

Valentine's Day is considered to be a most efficacious time for divining a future love. On this night, to see in a dream the face of one who will marry you, obtain two bay leaves. Sprinkle them with rose water and lay them (crossed over each other) under your pillow. As you lie down for the evening, say

> *Good Valentine*
> *Be kind to me,*
> *In dreams let me*
> *My true love see.*

A dream will reveal the face of your future spouse.

A related practice makes use not of plants but a mirror. On the first day of May in which the moon hangs (in any phase) in the night sky, hide a small mirror on your person and go out to stare silently at the moon. Repeat this for nine consecutive nights. On the last night, place the mirror beneath your pillow to dream of a beloved. This seems to have been in use while the loved one was absent to determine her or his state of happiness.

The moon figures into many love dream oracles. On the night when the new moon is first visible in the sky, go out and look at it while saying:

> *New moon, new moon, I hail thee!*
> *By all the virtue in thy body,*
> *Grant this night that I may see*
> *He who my true love is to be.*

She or he will appear in a dream that night.

On seven consecutive nights, count seven stars. Go to sleep. On the seventh night, you'll see the man or woman that you'll marry.

Or, walk into the night when the sky is clear. Stare at the brightest star that you can find. Wink three times and go to bed. A dream will be produced.

A lemon divination: remove the peel from two lemons. Place these in a small piece of cheesecloth and slip this packet inside your night clothes. If you dream of your desired one presenting you with two lemons, he or she surely loves you.

Pluck nine leaves from a smooth (that is, non-prickly) holly bush. Tie these up in a scarf with nine knots. Place this beneath your pillow and sleep. You will dream of your future partner that night.

And finally, cut an apple in half on the night of the full moon. Eat one half before midnight and the other half just after the clock strikes twelve (or, in today's world, when the liquid crystal numbers switch to 12:00 A.M.). Sleep and you'll dream of your love.

Paper

Some love divinations don't depend on dreams themselves to produce the response, but on sleep. Write the names of three possible future spouses on three pieces of paper. Fold each twice and place them under your pillow. Immediately remove one slip of paper before sleeping (do not read it). On waking the next morning, remove yet another slip. The remaining paper reveals the best possible choice.

The Apple

The apple is an extraordinary fruit. It has played a role in the mythologies of many European countries, and has found its way into innumerable love divinations. Here are just a few of them. (Divination with apples for other reasons will be found in Chapter 11: Plants and Herbs.)

Cut an apple in half. Count the number of seeds that you find inside it. If this number is even, marriage is in the offing. If an odd number, not. If one of the seeds has been accidentally cut in half, the road of romance will be somewhat rocky.

Similarly, to discover whether someone truly loves you, throw two apple seeds into a fire while saying:

> *If you love me, pop and fly;*
> *If you hate me, lie and die.*

If, while burning, the apple seeds make a sharp crackling sound, the person does have affection toward you. If no sound is made, no affection is felt.

An old practice involves discovering the initial of one's future spouse. Stand before a mirror. Stick an apple seed to your forehead. Immediately begin saying the alphabet. The letter at which the seed falls off reveals that person's initial. If you get through the entire alphabet and the seed hasn't dropped, no response is possible at this time.

A related practice involves naming two seeds for two specific possible spouses and sticking them to your forehead. The seed that remains the longest indicates that the person named for that seed is indeed in love with you.

A fourth method of apple-seed divination seems to have been first recorded in England in 1844, but is probably of earlier origin. Place an apple seed between the thumb and forefinger. Say the following:

> *Kernel come kernel, hop over my thumb,*
> *And tell me which way my true love will come,*
> *East, west, north, or south,*
> *Kernel jump into my true love's mouth.*

The seed is then squeezed hard between the fingers. The direction in which the pip flies at this pressure indicates the location of the future love. (This was most probably of the greatest use in small villages, where few persons would live in any direction and, thus, there were fewer possible lovers. Today it would be of little practical value.)

There are many more apple rites, but we'll end with just one more. This divination uses both the fruit and a mirror, and was often performed on Halloween—considered an efficacious time for love divination of all types.

After dusk, place a candle before a mirror. Stand before the mirror so that you can look into your reflection. Eat an apple and brush your hair. In time, your future lover will appear to be reflected in the mirror, peering eerily at you over your shoulder.

Basil Leaf Divination

Obtain two fresh basil leaves. Name one for yourself and one for your intended. Place them on a fire. If they lie still and don't burn, or burn slowly and/or silently, love is strong. If, however, they burn quickly, snapping and popping, a fight between the two of you may soon occur.

Straw

Find a piece of dried straw. Pinch it at one end while saying "Loves me." Pinch next to it and say "Loves me not." Continue until you've pinched the entire straw. The last statement is the true one.

Mistletoe

This is another plant that has long been associated with both love and magic. Save mistletoe after it's been taken down once Yule is past. Keep it carefully all year. When in the next December it is time to hang up another bunch, burn the now-dried mistletoe in a fire. If it burns with a steady flame, your future mate will be steady and true. If it crackles and splutters, she or he will be of a bad temperament. Alternately, place fresh or dried mistletoe under your pillow to dream of a future love.

The Ladybug

Though it's never permissible to kill a ladybug, you can ask it to determine the location of your love. Capture one as it rests on a leaf. Ask the creature to reveal the location of your true love. The direction in which it flies off reveals this information. Or, if the ladybug seems content to sit on your finger or hand for a few moments, count the spots that speckle its wings. If the number is even, you are certainly loved. If odd, not.

The Bulb of Love

Finally, we'll end with a rite that utilizes a flower bulb. Any type of flower may be used. This is best done in the spring. When you're unsure of the love of a spouse or other mate, plant the bulb in a pot filled with the appropriate soil mixture. Water it and care for it as usual. If it seems to sprout more quickly than normal, the signs are favorable. Keep watching it. If it blooms, the one that you love certainly loves you. If not, love hazards may be ahead.

15

Mirrors

As previously mentioned, mirrors have long played a vital role in the divinatory arts. Made of polished stone, burnished metal or glass, they're permanent versions of the original mirrors—still lakes.

Until the fourteenth century, humans were rarely certain of their own appearance. Only descriptions from others, paintings, dim reflections from water, or unsatisfactory mirrors gave them a clue as to this quite important information. Until that century, when glass mirrors were finally produced in Italy, we had great difficulty in attempting to live up to certain aspects of the ancient axiom: "Know thyself."

Mirror symbolism is based on reflection. Mirrors are symbolic of water, emblematic of the moon, which reflects the sun's light, and of enlightenment. Some of the early mystery religions are said to have used mirrors in their secret rites: they were presented to the candidate at a dramatic moment during initiation.

The divinatory use of true mirrors, as opposed to the use of other reflective surfaces, is of ancient origin. Metal mirrors were employed in ancient Greece, Rome, China, India, and elsewhere. Mirrors of obsidian were relied upon as scrying tools by the Aztecs in preconquest Mexico.

Mirror divination was quite popular in ancient Rome. Experts in this art were known as *specularii* and often performed their rites in the nude. A temple of Ceres at Patras was famous for the mirror divinations performed in a fountain that sat beside it. In Greece, the witches of Thessaly were said to be particularly fond of mirror divination.

Mirror gazing also found wide popularity throughout Europe at an early age. Though gazing into mirrors was constantly denounced by the church in the first thousand years of the current era, there were endless cases of religious persons, even church officials, who utilized them. One bishop of Verona was discovered to keep a mirror, inscribed on the back with the word *fiore* (flower), under his pillow. He was put to death for this heresy.

Today, when glass mirrors are cheaply produced, we haven't yet lost our mystical attitude toward these ubiquitous instruments—witness the supposed seven or nine years of bad luck that are said to follow the accidental breakage of a mirror. Mirrors continue to be used in the magical and divinatory arts, and there are no signs that this will soon change.

The mystery and lure of the mirror is quite plain: it reveals what we cannot see in any other way. Though it can show us a great deal, it remains physically empty. Its view of the world is the reverse of what we can see with our eyes. In spite of our current scientific knowledge of light waves, reflection is still considered to be a somewhat eerie phenomenon.

The information contained in this chapter is of both practical and historical value. Some of the ancient methods of creating and using mirrors would be difficult to put into practice today. Still, they form a part of the vast store of mirror lore, and represent many unique methods of determining the unknown.

Types of Magic Mirrors

The first European mirrors seem to have been made of highly polished metal—brass or silver were particularly favored. Before divinatory use, they were moistened with oil or water to improve their reflective properties. Even then, these mirrors produced poorly defined reflections. Such mirrors were used for grooming purposes as well as for divination. Other cultures used stone mirrors. These were, anciently, the only two forms of artificial mirrors—as opposed to natural mirrors, such as lakes.

Even after glass mirrors were available, however, a number of specialized metal mirrors were used in divination. These were related to the planets and had to be made at auspicious astrological moments. Each was used on a specific day and was consulted concerning specific subjects:

The Sun mirror was made of gold. It was used on Sundays to discover information concerning authority figures and those in power.

The Moon mirror was made of silver. Consulted on Mondays, it was useful for determining the likelihood of wishes manifesting in the future and for dream interpretation.

The Mercury mirror consisted of a globe of glass filled with mercury (the liquid metal). It was used on Wednesdays to discover the answers to inquiries regarding money and business ventures.

The Venus mirror was composed of copper. On Fridays, the diviner gazed at it to determine questions regarding love.

The Mars mirror was made of iron. It was consulted on Tuesdays for advice concerning arguments, lawsuits and other similar situations.

The Saturn mirror was composed of lead. Used on Saturday, it revealed lost articles and uncovered secrets.

Other forms of mirrors were also made and used. One common type consisted of glass globes that were filled with various substances and placed, cork downward, on a table. One of these was filled with pure water. A sort of artificial crystal ball, it was used as a gazing object. Recent books recommend creating similar globes, though most advise that the water be dyed blue or black.

An alternate form of these mirror globes was known as the narcotic mirror. This consisted of water in which powdered narcotic herbs such as belladonna, poppy, hemp, and henbane were mixed. The herbs were probably added to the water to mysteriously increase the globe mirror's effectiveness. This water, it should be noted, wasn't imbibed.

Modern divinatory mirrors take many forms. One of the commonest consists of a clock glass (or any similar round, concave piece of glass) painted on the convex side with black paint. This allows the unpainted glass to provide a reflective surface. The mirror is held in black velvet and acts as a gazing tool.

In the Ozarks, witches were thought to use a square or rectangular mirror framed on just three sides. This mirror had the power to show its user the doings of her or his enemies. The recommended three-sided frame was probably related to the moon (the three phases). Such mirrors were effective only when secret words were spoken during their use.

Perhaps the simplest of all divinatory mirrors consists of a plain piece of black paper inserted in a frame. No glass is used. A square frame is useful for obtaining knowledge of the physical world, while a round frame is most suited for information related to metaphysics and the spiritual world. This mirror is used as a tool of gazing.

Uses of Divinatory Mirrors

This form of mirror gazing can also be classified as hydromancy, as it utilizes water. Take a glass mirror to a lake, pond, or stream. Ask a question that can be answered with yes or no. Dip the mirror completely into the water three times, retrieving it each time. As you bring it up the last time, look into its mirrored surface. If your reflection is clear, the answer is yes. If it's distorted, the answer is the reverse. (This can also be performed by dipping a small mirror into a large bowl or bucket of water, or even in the bathtub before bathing.) If performing this at a well, it may be necessary to suspend the mirror from a string before lowering it into the water.

To inquire after the state of a loved one or family member, place a mirror so that it only reflects the ceiling. Light the room with white candles. Sit before the mirror. Gaze into it and ask "How is (name)?" An image of the person in question will eventually appear. If she or he seems to be smiling, all is well. If frowning, all is not well. If no expression is visible, or the face doesn't appear, no answer can be given at this time.

A curious ritual for divining the future is to be used on New Year's Eve. Go to an empty building. Sit on the floor. Place one mirror behind you and one in front of you. Each should be laid flat on the floor. Light a candle and place it between yourself and the mirror before you. At the stroke of midnight, gaze into the candle's flame as it is reflected on the mirror.

To know if an expected event will actually occur, use a grease pencil to write the question on a small mirror. Wrap this in several layers of cloth, place it beneath your pillow, and sleep on it. If you dream of the hoped-for event, it will occur. If not, it probably won't.

Finally, take a mirror to a window on a day and at a time when the sun shines into the house. Hold the mirror so that it reflects the sun's light onto the ceiling. Watch the moving patterns that this reflection creates and see symbols of the future.

16

Stars, the Moon,
and Lightning

The mysterious lights that brighten the night sky have long been viewed with superstitious awe. They were believed to be the souls of the dead, the abodes of the deities, even missiles (shooting stars) hurled toward earth. Usually, though, stars are considered to be mysterious yet friendly lights capable of predicting events in the human existence. Astrology is but one ancient divinatory practice linked with the stars.

Many cultures have built crude calendars based on the reappearance of stars after their yearly departures. The rising of the North Star, Sirius, predicted the annual inundation of the Nile in ancient Egypt. In Hawaii, this same star first appearing again in the sky marked the beginning of a four-month festival. Many constellations that we no longer recognize enjoyed prestige as omens of events that were about to occur.

The sight of a comet has long been viewed as the most ominous of star omens. They were virtually always seen as predictions of disaster: the fall of kings and queens; the destruction of cities; even the end of the world. Some disasters did follow the sighting of comets; thus, this belief continued for thousands of years.

Pliny, the Roman naturalist who died in C.E. 79 when his curiosity concerning the erupting Mt. Vesuvius led him to stray too close to its poisonous fumes and falling ashes, wrote extensively about comets in his famous *Natural History*. He wrote of several types, the "horned" comet, "torch" comet, the "goat" comet, and many others, each described according to its appearance. Certain types of comets portended specific influences. One shaped like a pair of flutes predicted success in the arts, while a specific comet that appeared during Augustus Caesar's reign had a health-giving influence over the entire globe. However, most considered comets to be omens of ill luck.

Shooting stars are other dramatic signs of future ills or joys. Meteorites were worshipped as deities in China, Rome, and elsewhere. In weather lore, they've been seen to predict hurricanes, yet in England a woman desiring to bear a child looked anxiously at the sky; the sight of a meteorite flashing through the night was a sure sign that she would become pregnant. In other parts of England the sight of a shooting star was a certain sign of an impending marriage.

Star Divinations

Many forms of divination still in use today rely on the stars. Even dreaming of stars is considered to be an omen of future happiness. Here are some of these techniques:

- Go outside at night when the sky is clear. Ask a question. If the stars seem to glow brighter, or if a shooting star races across the sky, the answer is yes. If nothing seems to occur after fifteen minutes, or if clouds blot out the stars, the response is no.

- Before going to bed, walk outside, look up at the sky and say the following: "Stars, stars, show me the future." It will appear in a dream that night.

- Wishing on a star is a popular practice. Outside, look at one particular star for several minutes. State your hoped-for future. Close your eyes for three seconds. If, upon opening your eyes, they immediately fix on the same star, your future is as you wished. If you can't find it at once, your future will be different.

The Moon

The moon is an old friend in divination. Associated with goddesses and gods, dragons, rabbits, frogs, mice, and other creatures, the moon's pale light and various shapes have foretold many things. The moon is closely linked with dreams (which it is sometimes thought to produce) and the sea. Here are a few simple lunar divinations:

On the new moon (that is, when the moon first appears in the sky as a thin crescent), go outside and point a dull-bladed knife (preferably silver) at the moon. Say the following words:

> *New moon, true morrow, be true now to me*
> *That I ere the morrow my true love may see.*

Place the knife beneath your pillow. Speak to no one as you prepare for bed. Remember your dreams.

The position of the moon on the evening that you first spot it is considered to be of importance. When you first see the moon after her change (the new moon) directly before you or on your right side, the month will be of the utmost good fortune. If, however, you happen to see the moon over your left shoulder, or if you have to turn your head behind you to see it, the month will be decidedly less lucky.

To produce a dream of future events hold a piece of silver up to the moon at the time of its full phase. Ask your question, return home and place the silver beneath your pillow. If the query is to come true in the near future you'll dream of it that night.

On the night of the moon's reappearance after her period of retiring, say the following directly to the lunar orb:

> *New moon, true moon,*
> *Star in the stream,*
> *Pray tell me my fortune*
> *In my dream.*

At one time, the day of the moon (not the day of the week) upon which a person was born indicated that person's future life and character. Each of the twenty-eight days of the lunar calendar also betokened specific influences. This is a crude form of astrology that anyone could practice. Here, in a highly abbreviated form, is one common European version of this ancient form of divination:

Day One (that is, the new moon): A person who is born on this day will have a long life and be happy.

Day Two: Finances may be a problem for those born on this day.

Day Three: An inauspicious day upon which to be born.

Day Four: Political success is assured for those born on this day.

Day Five: No omens concerning birth. However, it is very fortunate for women to conceive on this day.

Day Six: A child born on this day will become a skilled hunter.

No omens for days seven through nine.

Tenth Day: A person born on this day will travel widely, but will never achieve lasting tranquility.

No omens for days eleven through twenty.

Twenty-First Day: A child born on this day may become a thief.

No omens for days twenty-two through twenty-eight.

Similar systems were in use in Hawaii and elsewhere. Unfortunately, few remain in their original, complete forms. Time has taken its toll.

Lightning

Lightning is one of the most powerful of all natural forces. Though each bolt or flash lasts for just tenths of a second, the undeniable power unleashed by this phenomena has permanently imprinted it within the human mind as being highly portentous of future events. Most cultures viewed lightning in this manner.

The Greeks associated lightning with male deities. According to Pliny, lightning that occurred during the day was produced by Jupiter, while night lightning was the handiwork of the god Summanus (an epithet of Poseidon). Lightning was thought to consist of fiery bolts thrown down by these gods. Though some South American cultures believed that the moon created lightning, most others associated it with the sun.

The earliest source of fire was almost assuredly trees that had been fortuitously struck by lightning. As they burned, early humans touched branches to the fire and thus preserved it for cooking and heating use. Lightning was sacred.

In ancient Rome, the appearance, proximity, and brightness of lightning foretold the future success or failure of a newly set up household. This prediction was effective for the first ten years. Lightning omens are known throughout the world.

There are a few specific provoked omens concerned with lightning. The first is perhaps the oldest. Go outside on a night that will probably bring a storm. Stand facing in any direction and wait for the first flash. If it appears to the left, it's a sign of trouble and heartaches. If, however, it appears on the right, this portends a happy, prosperous future. If it's directly overheard, a mixture of both. (This is also a sign that it might be best to take cover.) If you've asked a specific question it is answered in the same manner: to the left, no. To the right, yes. If it appears directly overhead, no answer is can be given at this time.

It is well-known that counting the seconds between a lightning flash and the thunder that it causes provides a crude method of determining its distance from the observer. To utilize this phenomenon in a divinatory manner, go outside after the first bolt. Ask a binary question. At the second flash, begin counting one one-thousand, two one-thousand, and so on. Stop counting as the thunder rumbles across the sky. If the number that you've reached is even, the answer is yes. If odd, no.

17

Other Forms of Divination

This chapter includes a variety of techniques that don't seem to fit anywhere else.

Cloth

This seems to have been of Roman origin. Collect several small pieces of cloth, preferably of the same type of material (check with a friend who sews, or purchase remnants at a fabric shop). One of each of the following colors is required: yellow, red, gray, blue, green, black, and orange.

Cut each piece of fabric into small squares of uniform size, perhaps two inches square. Place them in a box. For a general divination, mix them up, reach into the box and draw one out at random. The color chosen determines the future:

Yellow: Jealousy.

Red: Love, fortune, success.

Gray: Inaction, delay.

Blue: Health, peace, happiness.

Green: Money.

Black: Sadness, trouble.

Orange: Misfortune.

Pieces of paper of these colors can be substituted for the cloth squares.

Eggs

The origin of using eggs in divination (known variously as *ovoscopy, ovomancy,* or *oomantia*) has been lost. Though eggs can be used in a number of ways to determine the future, one method is best-known, and is used throughout Europe to this day.

Fill a clear, tall glass with water. Using a pin, prick a hole in the egg's smaller end. Hold the egg over the water until the white begins to drip from it into the glass. Ask a question, if any.

Watch as the egg whites diffuse and create shapes as they hang and float in the water. These are usually quite fantastic in appearance. From these shapes and through the use of symbolic thought, determine the future.

A second method is more delicious. Hard-boil seven eggs in the usual manner. Allow them to cool in the water. Then, using combinations of food colorings in water (or the dyes available for this purpose in the spring), dye each egg one of these colors: red, orange, yellow, green, blue, and purple. Leave the seventh egg white.

Once the dyes have dried place the eggs in a bowl. Ask your question. Close your eyes and select one egg at random from the bowl. Read the future according to the following interpretations:

Red: Things are moving; beware.

Orange: Great change is ahead, either positive or negative.

Yellow: Thought will be necessary; don't rely on emotions.

Green: You'll be entering a creative period; a positive sign.

Blue: Love and relationships are forecast.

Purple: Higher forces are at work.

White: No response is possible at this time.

Another version utilizes three eggs, but here their colors' meanings are altered. Dye one dark blue, one orange, and leave the third white. Place them in a bowl and, with your eyes closed, mix them around with your hands. Ask a yes/no question. Choose an egg:

Dark blue: No.

Orange: Yes.

White: No answer is possible at this time.

Kites

Those of us with fond memories of flying kites on blustery spring days may be surprised at their ancient history. They probably were invented in China. Marco Polo noted seeing the wondrous instruments during his travels throughout this huge country.

Their origin is lost, but kites may have been sophisticated versions of banners. The addition of a string was all that was necessary to create kites. Most Chinese kites were made of bamboo and paper or silk, and were ingeniously fashioned in the forms of hawks and other types of birds, caterpillars, lizards, goats, butterflies, octopi, and snakes.

Hawaiians, who must have picked up the idea from their Polynesian ancestors who originated in Asia, envisioned one of their deities, Lolupe, in the form of a stingray-shaped kite. Kite flying was a cherished pastime in the islands.

Kites had many uses in ancient China. They were weapons in fighting contests (the object was to bring down the other kite); scarecrows to frighten away birds; observation posts (men were hoisted into the air on kites to determine the enemy's movements) and tools of divination. Kites were even used as scapegoats: misfortunes were piled into the kite, it was sent into the air and the string was cut to release the ills.

Kites were introduced to Europe in the 1700s, and soon the custom of kite flying spread throughout the world. Kite flying has become such an integral part of spring activities in our country that many believe kites to be American inventions.

The divinatory uses of kites are difficult to find. Certainly, the direction of the wind can be easily determined by the movement of kites, and this can be a sign of the future. Still, much of this lore has been lost. One of the few kite divinations recorded from earlier times doesn't depend on the wind for predictions.

In Morocco, as late as the early 1900s, young women would fly kites from the rooftops. If they flew strong and well, the omen was positive. However, if the string broke during the flight, dire misfortune had been predicted. Having the string become entangled in nearby electrical wires or trees was similarly inauspicious.

This same system can be used to answer binary questions. If the kite flies well, the answer is yes. If the string breaks or becomes entangled, no.

Knives

The shimmering blades of knives held opposite flames were once used as gazing tools. The fire's reflection produced symbolic responses.

A more modern form of knife divination is often used to determine the direction from which troubles stem. Place a knife on a table and ensure that it easily spins. State your question and vigorously spin the knife by its middle. The direction to which the blade points indicates from where the misfortunes are emanating. This can also be tried to find an object has been lost in the house. For this purpose, the tip will point to its hiding place.

A second method of consulting the knife oracle consists of creating a circle of small pieces of paper on which you've written each of the letters of the alphabet, from A to Z. Place the knife in the exact center of the circle, its sharp tip pointing away from you. Ask a question and spin the knife by grasping its middle and giving it a twist. The letter to which the knife's sharp tip points determines the response. If the first letter indicated by the knife is "Y," you need not continue; the question has been answered (yes). If an "N," the answer is no. If neither of these two letters turn up, continue asking the same question and spin the knife a total of thirteen times (keep track of the letters in the correct order between spins). These may spell out words that reveal the future. You may have to jumble around the letters a bit to receive a clear understanding of the message.

Needles and Pins

Though needles and pins have an ancient history, only when they began to be made of lightweight metal did they become popular tools of divination. Needle and pin divinations are known the world over.

A European version: place twenty-five needles on a plate. Pour water over the plate, until the needles float. If any of the needles cross, the future looks ill. If, however, none cross, all will be fine.

After exposure to western European ways, Cherokee shamans also used pins in divination.

The Cherokee used needles to determine the prognosis of ill clients. A new white bowl, eight inches in diameter, was filled with water. After a prayer, two pins were floated on the water (in the manner described in the next paragraph) about two inches apart. If the needles maintained this distance or moved farther apart, the client would recover. If the left needle drifted toward the right needle, a poor prognosis had been made; she or he might not be healed.

Another method is also based on a Cherokee technique. Collect water from a flowing stream. Pour this into a vessel. Ask a yes or no question. Place a needle on the middle finger of your right hand. Slowly dip your hand into the water until the needle floats on its surface. Watch the needle. If it floats for a long time, the future is positive or the answer is yes. If it quickly sinks, the omen is negative or the answer is no.

Pins find fewer divinatory applications, but they can be useful in determining the sex of an unborn child. This technique is closely related to the use of a pendulum. Attach a pin to a thread. Hold this over the pregnant woman's wrist or her stomach. If the suspended pin swings in a clockwise direction, it will be a boy. If counterclockwise, a girl will shortly arrive.

In England, unmarried women visited wells and dropped pins into them. If the pins floated, the diviner was loved. If they sank, she was not loved. This method can also be used to answer all types of binary questions: floating signifies yes; sinking, no.

Oil

As mentioned in Chapter 2, oil divination (lecanomancy) was widely practiced in Babylon and in many ancient cultures. A special class of divinatory priests were expert in this art, and we can glean much from their practices.

You'll need a bowl of water and a jar of olive oil. Put the bowl on a table and sit before it. Ask for a general reading of the future and slowly pour a bit of the oil into the water. A teaspoon or so is sufficient. The oil will rise and float on the water's surface. Watch it for a few moments. Determine the future according to the following list:

- If the oil divides into two sections, an argument may be in the offing—or a negative answer.

- If the oil forms a ring (not a filled circle) and this remains unbroken, a business journey will be profitable, or the sick will recover—or a positive response.

- If smaller droplets of oil emerge from a larger one, it may indicate pregnancy. This is also a favorable sign for the sick, for it predicts recovery.

- If oil spreads thinly and covers the entire surface of the water, beware—troubles are ahead.

- Many small, unconnected globules of oil indicate the coming of money.

- A crescent or a star shape is extremely fortunate.

A similar method still in use is a form of scrying (gazing). Sit at a table before the bowl of fresh water. A candle should be the only source of illumination. Ask your question or simply clear your mind. Pour oil into the water until it forms a circle on its surface. Gaze into the flickering reflection of the candle's flame on the oil and determine the future. In Italy, this is most often used to divine whether a spell had been cast against either the diviner or the person for whom the rite was performed. However, it can be used for a variety of other divinatory purposes.

Another method also stems from Italy. Fill a bowl with water. Add a quantity of olive oil as well as a great deal of ground black pepper. Place a few fingers into the bowl and swirl it around in all directions, so that some of the pepper adheres to the sides of the bowl above the surface of the water. Ask your question while performing this. Stop, remove your fingers and interpret the symbols created by the pepper blots in the manner of tea-leaf readers.

Paper

At one time, paper was enormously expensive, due to the work that went into its manufacture. (The same was true of the Middle Eastern variety, papyrus.) Some cultures actually punished the deliberate wasting of paper. As paper decreased in value many found it to be an excellent tool of divination. It often replaced earlier objects (such as leaves) used in the prophetic arts. Paper's unique ability to be folded, ripped, and written upon made it a natural tool. Many of the techniques described elsewhere in this book use paper (see index). Here we'll describe just three others.

Write questions on five small pieces of paper. Roll them up into tight cylinders. Place these in a metal strainer and hold it in the steam rising from a pot on the stove (or a fire). The first of these to unroll has been affirmatively answered; the others questions, no.

The second method is even simpler. Cut two squares of the same size from the same piece of white paper. Using a black marking pen or ink, color one piece of paper black. Go to an upstairs window and, asking your question, at the same time throw the squares out of the window. Carefully observe which square lands first on the ground: this determines the answer. If it is black, the answer is yes. If white, no. (Retrieve the slips of paper and dispose of them properly.)

Or, cut a five-pointed star from a piece of paper. On each leg, write one of the following: "yes," "no," "maybe," "probably." Leave the fifth leg blank. Write lightly with a pencil, not a pen; you shouldn't be able to read the answers when the paper is turned blank-side-down.

Ask your question. Place the star under your pillow face-down. Each evening for four nights, fold over one leg of the star without turning it over to see which answer has been eliminated. On the fifth night look to see which corner hasn't been folded. This will answer your question.

Pearls

Margaritomancy is a curious form of divination that uses pearls, which were originally consulted to determine the name of a thief. The names of the suspected persons were read off and the pearl responded in a dramatic way at the mention of the guilty party's name.

This version is more useful. Place an unstrung pearl on the hearth before a roaring fire. Cover this with an upside-down metal bowl. State a series of questions, each of which can be answered with a yes or no response. Such questions might include "Will I find a love within the next six months?" "Will my new job be fulfilling and financially rewarding?" and so on.

If the bowl remains silent while each question is asked, none will come true in the near future. A positive response is gathered when, while a question is being asked, the pearl rises and strikes the bowl's interior, creating a hollow ringing sound. I don't know anyone who's actually tried this divination, as few of us have unstrung pearls lying around the house. However, if you do, it might be worth trying. It certainly remains one of the most mysterious of all divinations.

Pendulums

The use of a pendulum is related to dowsing, in which a tool dips downward when the dowser passes over the material for which she or he is searching (see the article that discusses *rhabdomancy* in Appendix 1: A Dictionary of Divinations). It's also related to dactylomancy and other methods. While this method of divination has its limitations (as discussed below), it can be of assistance.

A pendulum consists of nothing more than a heavy object suspended from a string. It's generally used today to answer yes or no questions, though in the past pendulums were often called upon to determine the sex of unborn children. Some dowsers supplement their outdoor activities with pendulums held over maps. This allows them to cover a far larger area than would be otherwise possible.

Pendulums also have their therapeutic applications. Some specialists will hold a pendulum over various homeopathic remedies to determine the best one to prescribe. Others will perform a similar technique over various types of food.

Virtually any small object that can be tied to a string can be used as the required weight. Pierced stones, buttons, coins, and rings are some popular choices; the Cherokee of

North America used arrowheads. Attach the object to a natural-fiber string of about six to eight inches in length. Elaborate, showy pendulums are available in some metaphysical supply stores, but these are usually expensive and won't necessarily produce better results. Use what you have.

To use the pendulum, sit at a table. Rest the elbow of your writing hand on the table and hold the end of the string between your thumb and forefinger. Ask a question that can be answered affirmatively or negatively. Hold your arm and the string perfectly still and wait.

The pendulum will begin to swing. There are two differing methods of interpreting these movements. The first is perhaps the easiest to remember. If the pendulum swings in a circle either clockwise or counterclockwise, the answer is yes; if in a back-and-forth motion, no. If it refuses to move, no answer can be produced.

The second method of interpreting the pendulum's movements involves only circular motion. A clockwise circle is yes; a counterclockwise motion, no.

To discover the pendulum's preferred method of responses, ask it a question that you already know the answer to. If you're a woman, ask "Am I a woman?" If it moves in a circular motion, then ask "Am I a man?" If it moves counterclockwise, utilize the second set of interpretations. If it moves back and forth, the first method.

Some people believe that the subconscious mind is responsible for the pendulum's movements. This certainly seems to be true. Thus, its ability to foretell our futures is limited. It can't predict major events (which may be caused by a number of outside factors). Still, as a tool of contacting the subconscious mind, the pendulum has proven effective more often than not.

Rings

Divination with rings, known as *dactylomancy*, is closely related to the pin rite mentioned above. It is of ancient origin though the modern version has been greatly simplified. In the Middle Ages, specially crafted rings were in vogue for this form of divination. Each was appropriate for use in dactylomancy on a particular day of the week:

Sun: Made from gold, this ring bore a peridot carved with the image of a lion-headed snake. Used on Sunday.

Moon: The ring of this luminary was made of silver and set with quartz crystal that had been engraved with two crescents. Used on Monday.

Mars: Made of iron, bearing a ruby displaying the image of a serpent biting a sword's hilt. Used on Tuesday.

Mercury: Fashioned of tin or lead. It bore a carnelian engraved with a caduceus (a wand entwined with two serpents). Used on Wednesday.

Jupiter: Tin set with a topaz engraved with an eagle and a five-pointed star constituted this ring. Used on Thursday.

Venus: Made of copper, this ring was set with an emerald and carved with a symbol of sexual union. Used on Friday.

Saturn: Made of lead and set with an onyx bearing the image of a snake encircling a stone. Used on Saturday.

To actually use the rings, each letter of the alphabet was engraved on three metal discs. The seventy-eight discs were placed on a round table marked with the signs of the zodiac and the planets. A ring of the appropriate metal was suspended from a linen thread, which was held over the table.

After prayer, a consecrated torch was applied to the thread. As the thread burned, the ring fell on to the table. This process was repeated seven times. Those letters over which the ring rolled and the one on which it halted were grouped together to form a response to the question.

The modern method is far simpler. Attach a thread to a ring—gold wedding rings are preferred, but any can be used. Suspend this in an empty glass. Ask your question. If the ring knocks against the glass only once, the answer is yes. If twice, no. (Wait a few moments after the first knocking to see if another will follow.)

Alternately, observe the direction in which the ring hits the glass. If it knocks against the left side, the omen is bad; if to the right side, good; against the far side of the glass, bad; against the near side, good.

Sand

Sand divination is another ancient art. Obtain a quantity of fine sand. If it's damp, bake it in an oven until the moisture has been evaporated by the heat. Pour it into a square or rectangular tray to the depth of three inches. Place this on a table before you.

Hold a pencil loosely in your hand and place its point on the center of the sand. Close your eyes and state your question. Breathe deeply and relax.

You'll have a strong urge to move the pencil. Let it move of its own accord across and through the sand. Continue this until the pencil stops moving, or in about three minutes, whichever comes first. A longer period of writing may create a jumble of confusing messages incapable of interpretation.

Remove the pencil and look down at the symbols on the sand. Sometimes, legible words will be created by the pencil's movement. There may also be a "Y" for yes, an "N" for no, or a "P" for perhaps. More usually, symbols will appear. Some of those most commonly seen in sand divination include:

Large circle: Misfortune.

Small circle: News, especially pertaining to work.

Triangle: Success.

Square: Obstacles.

A long line: A journey.

A short line: A visitor.

Heart: Love, relationships, friendships.

Broken or uneven heart: Partings.

Flower: Beginnings.

An "X": Love.

If other symbols appear, interpret them with your question in mind.

An alternate form of sand reading: pour fine sand into a sieve. Shake this over a flat, light-colored surface while asking your question. Gaze into the patterns created by the sand as it falls onto the surface. Use symbolic thought to decode their messages.

Part III

Advanced Techniques

18

Tarot

Though the precise origins of both playing cards and the Tarot are unknown, no cards have survived from truly ancient cultures. The Tarot—a deck of cards used in divination—is of fairly recent origin, perhaps during the thirteenth century in Europe. However, this hasn't stopped latter-day commentators from creating fantastic stories concerning its origins: that it originally appeared as seventy-eight paintings inside the Great Pyramid, that it had some connection with the Eleusinian mysteries, that it is a text from Atlantis, that it stems from ancient Babylon, and so on.

Such beliefs aside, it's likely that, far from a mysterious origin, the Tarot was invented for educational Christian purposes, for gambling, or for pure amusement. Divinatory practices with the Tarot were a later development.

The earliest surviving specimens of Tarot cards, housed in the *Bibliotheque Nationale,* were painted by Gringon-neur for the amusement of the mad King Charles VI of France in 1392. Court accounts of the period record a payment to Jaquemin Gringonneur for three sets of Tarot cards—the Major Arcana only.

Regular playing cards first made an appearance in literature in 1332, when Alfonse XI banned their use. A German
monk, Johannes, wrote of the use of playing cards in his
monastery in the year 1377. He states that they had value
in teaching Christian morality to others.

At this period of time, there was no agreement concerning the designs of either playing cards or the Tarot. Each
deck both resembled and differed from others.

Beginning in the fifteenth century, the Gypsies spread
knowledge of the Tarot use wherever they roamed in Europe—but they neither invented them nor first introduced
them to the continent.

Finally, in the late 1700s, the Tarot was used solely as a
tool of divination. (This may have occurred earlier, but we
have no records to support this.)

The Modern Revival

Tarot cards, once the sole province of Gypsies, underwent
a revival of interest when, in 1910, A. E. Waite and Pa-
mela Colman Smith created what is known as the Waite
or Rider-Waite deck. This was the first modern deck and
formed the basis for the countless ones that followed.
Drawing from a number of sources, Waite directed Smith
to include a great deal of symbolism in the cards. Some of
this imagery was undoubtedly traditional, some was bor-
rowed from initiatory organizations, and some of it was
probably pure Waite.

The tradition of creating Tarot decks is still quite alive.
There are now decks flavored with Mayan, American In-
dian, Aztec and feminist themes, Celtic decks, Wiccan

packs, mythological sets, those concerned solely with "cat-people," and many, many others. Some persons collect Tarot decks old and new. Even the famous surrealist Salvador Dali designed and painted an entire Tarot deck.

As the popularity of the Tarot continues, writers and artists have continually altered the designs found on the cards, thus changing their divinatory meanings. Most new decks contain a small booklet describing each card's symbolism and predictive qualities. Though some general similarities exist, most authors don't agree with each other. Thus, each card has a huge range of potential meanings.

Most experts recommend the Rider-Waite deck when first beginning to use the cards. This was once necessary: it was the only deck that was widely available. Today, students who are offended by the Christian symbolism and sexist undertones of this deck can choose from a variety of others.

The Deck

The Tarot consists of seventy-eight cards, which are divided into two decks: the twenty-two Major Arcana cards and the fifty-six minor arcana. The Minor Arcana closely corresponds to our modern playing cards; the Major Arcana is unique.

Unlike modern playing cards, which are double-headed, and thus are identical whether upside-down or right-side-up, the images on the Tarot can fall either way. "Reversed" interpretations are thus an important part of most Tarot readings. In general, upright cards are interpreted in positive ways; reversed cards in negative ways.

The Minor Arcana

The Minor Arcana, often considered to be of lesser divinatory importance than the Major Arcana, consists of four
suits of fourteen cards each: Ace through Ten, Knight, Page,
Queen, and King. In general, these suits are concerned with
the following matters:

Pentacles: The Earth, the material world, money, and
business.

Wands: Feelings, intellect, beginnings, direction, creation.

Cups: Water, intuition, emotions, love, lovemaking,
happiness.

Swords: Strife, strength, difficulties, challenges, energy.

These suits correspond to our playing cards in the following manner: Pentacles: Diamonds; Wands: Clubs; Cups:
Hearts; Swords: Spades.

In most pre-twentieth-century decks, the Minor Arcana
aren't as richly illustrated as the Major Arcana. This
has changed, however; many modern decks are fully illustrated. The Aces for each suit of the *Universal Tarot* (Lo
Scarabeo) deck are shown on the next page.

The Major Arcana

This consists of twenty-two cards (numbered 0 through
21, which often confuses those first using the cards). The
Major Arcana are sometimes seem as archetypes; at the
very least, they represent powerful influences.

The Major Arcana and each card's symbolism and potential divinatory meaning follow. This information is

based on a survey of the literature as well as personal experience; however, differences are to be found in many decks, and you may find a completely different meaning for some cards.

Some cards are known by different names in some decks: the High Priestess may be termed the Papess; the Hierophant as the Pope, and so on. The Major Arcana cards used to illustrate this section are from the *Universal Tarot* deck (reproduced with permission from Lo Scarabeo).

The Aces

0. The Fool
Upright: The subconscious mind.
Reversed: Negligence. Refusal to open one's eyes to see what lies ahead. Foolishness. Carelessness.

1. The Magician
Upright: Strength of will. Skill. Subtlety. Diplomacy. Mastery of natural forces.
Reversed: Use of powers for evil ends. Illusion. Insecurity.

2. The High Priestess

Upright: Knowledge. Secrets. Wisdom. intuition. Balance. Foresight. The future. Spiritual enlightenment. The female mysteries. Mystery traditions. Initiation. Natural forces.

Reversed: Ignorance. Superficiality. Surface knowledge. Wisdom used for unwise purposes.

3. The Empress

Upright: The Earth Mother. Motherhood. Emotions. Fertility (of all kinds). Sensuality.

Reversed: Domestic strife. Poverty. Fear. Anxiety. Indecision, but also possibly truth, light and rejoicing.

4. The Emperor
Upright: Competence. Worldly influence. Intelligence overcoming emotion. Realization of all goals. Protection. Authority.
Reversed: Immaturity. Weakness of character. Uncontrolled emotions. Loss of wealth. Lack of authority.

5. The Hierophant
Upright: A religious vocation. Teaching. Fatherhood. Mercy. Compassion. Ritual. Authority. A high priest.
Reversed: Misuse of spiritual authority. Control of others. Generosity to a fault. Unconventionality.

6. The Lovers

Upright: Love. Union. Beauty. Attraction. Reconciliation. Harmony.
Reversed: Infidelity. Unfulfilling relationships. Obsession with love object. Foolish plans.

7. The Chariot

Upright: Control of inner energies. Mastery of the elements. Obstacles that have been faced. Confrontations. Effort. Victory. Conquest.
Reversed: Failure to succeed. Defeat. Plans falling apart. Failure to face responsibility. Bad news will arrive. War and conflicts. Vengeance.

8. Strength

Upright: Fortitude. Energy. Hidden forces. Heroism. Physical and spiritual power. Vitality. Success. *Reversed:* Tyranny. Weakness. Discord. The abuse of power. Obstinacy and stubbornness. Disgrace. Danger.

9. The Hermit

Upright: The inner search for truth and wisdom. Circumspection. Thriftiness. Meditation. Withdrawal. Silence. The need for caution. Secrets will be revealed.

Reversed: Delays due to unreasonable caution. Fear. Loneliness. Fanaticism concerning a spiritual path. Disguise.

10. The Wheel of Fortune

Upright: Unexpected events. Cyclicity. Evolution. Fortune. Unforeseen change. Probability. Chaos. *Reversed:* Increase (some say poverty, fear, loneliness).

11. Justice

Upright: Absolute justice. Judgement. Impartiality. Virtue. Success in legal matters: lawsuits, wills, contracts. Balance. Karma.
Reversed: Unfair condemnation. Bigotry. Excessive severity. Bias. Intolerance. False accusations.

12. The Hanged Man
Upright: Initiation. Wisdom. The power of prophecy. Sacrifice necessary to obtain a goal. Divination. Transformation. Prophecy. Rebirth. Devotion.
Reversed: Unwillingness to make necessary sacrifices. Selfishness. Punishment. Loss. Enforced sacrifice. Defeat. Hypocrisy.

13. Death
Upright: Destruction, change and renewal. Major positive change in circumstances. Reincarnation (and, thus, events in past lives that affect this one). The death of old ideas and cherished beliefs.
Reversed: Stagnation, negative change. A major unfortunate change in circumstances. Ruin. Endings. (Note: virtually never refers to physical death.)

14. Temperance

Upright: Self-control. Moderation. Friendship. Fusion. Patience. Frugality. Working harmoniously with others. Mixation. Combination.
Reversed: Extravagance, perplexity, overindulgence, discord, inability to work with others.

15. The Devil

Upright: Unnecessary bondage to others, to concepts or material objects. Suffering. Violence. Delusion. Fear.
Reversed: Throwing off bondage. Overcoming fear and delusion. Finding path to enlightenment. Conquering base desires and beliefs. A controlled subconscious mind. (Example of how a reversed interpretation may be positive, etc.)

16. The Tower

Upright: Transformation of existing forms to make room for the new. Destruction. Violence. Overthrow. Loss. Reversal of fortune. Ambition. Tyranny.

Reversed: The same but to a lesser degree.

17. The Star

Upright: Hope. trust. optimism. Insight. Opportunity. Bright promises. A favorable future.

Reversed: Restriction. Self-doubt. Pessimism. Disappointment. Dreaminess. Unfulfilled hopes. Broken promises. Expectations dashed.

18. The Moon

Upright: Promise. Fulfillment. Women in general. Dreams. Twilight. Deception. Hidden enemies. Dissatisfaction. Lying. Trickery. Scandal. Revealed secrets. Mistakes.
Reversed: the same to a lesser degree.

19. The Sun

Upright: Fruitfulness. Sacred truth. Pleasure. Riches. Gain. Glory. Success in employment. Achievement. Recovery from sickness. Joy. Success. Happiness.
Reversed: Vanity. Shamelessness. Arrogance; the upright meanings in a minor degree.

20. Judgement

Upright: Rejuvenation. Rehabilitation. Recovery from addiction. Improvement in all things.

Reversed: Difficulty in coming to a decision. Maintaining old habits. Lack of positive change. Delay. The desire not to face facts.

21. The World

Upright: Success. Completion. Joy. Perfection. Attainment of all things. Triumph. Travel.

Reversed: Fear of change. Fear of success. Lack of vision. Inability to accept the positive.

Using the Tarot

Though a minimum of Tarot knowledge is presented here, this chapter would be incomplete without at least one method of using the cards for divinatory purposes. For further information, consult any of the books listed in the bibliography.

In divination, the Tarot is shuffled and cut. A card is chosen at random, or several cards are laid out in a pattern. The past, present, and/or future is determined by interpreting the cards' symbolism.

One method of consulting the Tarot is the easiest. Shuffle the cards as you concentrate on your question. Shuffle at least nine times. Lay the pack on a table and cut it. Shuffle once more. (There are many variations on this process.)

Select the top card. Carefully turn it over so that you don't accidentally invert it. Study the card's symbolism. Then, interpret the cards in relation to your question. That's the whole of it.

Of course, while this process is easily explained, it can be difficult to successfully practice. The Tarot is a complex tool that must be carefully studied to produce the best results. Below is a plan for familiarizing yourself with Tarot divination.

1. Find the most appealing Tarot deck. Many metaphysical shops have opened decks so that you can examine the cards contained within them. Choose the one that calls to you.

2. Set aside a certain period of time each day to study one Tarot card. Doing this with all of the cards will

require seventy-eight days. Don't look up the card's meaning in books—study the card itself. Become aware of its symbolism. Try to fit it into your daily life. It's best to note your observations for each card.

3. Read books on the subject, but realize that different books contain different interpretations. Compare the information contained within books to your own interpretations of the cards. Notice the similarities and differences and decide which are most appropriate. Your interpretations may well be the best for you.

4. Then, and only then, begin using the Tarot for divination. Attempting to do this before gaining knowledge of the deck is likely to end in failure, for you must become familiar with the tool before using it. Read only for yourself at first. Later, when you've gained proficiency, you can read for friends.

5. Keep studying and practicing. Respect the Tarot. Call upon it when in need, and remember: the future can be changed.

19

Palmistry

Palmistry (also known as *cheirognomy* and *cheiromancy*) is the art of determining character and the future by the study of the shape of the human hand as well as the lines that cross its palm. This practice, today usually associated with Gypsy fortunetellers, is quite old. Passages in the Vedas suggest its practice as early as 1000 B.C.E.

It was in Greece and Rome, however, that palmistry came to be regarded as a science. Many writers (including Aristotle, the Emperor Augustus, and Pliny) referred to this practice. From Rome the art was spread throughout the empire.

With the rise of Christianity, palmistry was persecuted and banned throughout Europe. It was lumped together with everything else that the Church didn't understand and labeled a demonic practice. Only those on the fringes of society dared to read hands, and then only in secrecy.

Finally, in the nineteenth century, palmistry emerged from the shadows and was once again regarded as a respectable art. Perhaps the most famous palmist and one of its more ardent defenders was the Count Louis Harmon, better known by the professional name of Cheiro. Cheiro operated reading rooms in both London and the United States. As word of his accuracy spread, he read the palms of the powerful, the rich, and the influential, while suffering from the criticisms of those who would link palmistry with the devil. Among the famous persons for whom he performed readings were Lord Kitchener, Mata Hari, Sarah Bernhardt, Oscar Wilde, King Edward VIII of England, Mark Twain, and Lillian Gish.

Cheiro wrote a series of books detailing his personal system of reading hands. In many ways his techniques differed from those who had come before him, but his works enjoyed tremendous popularity and still form the basis of cheiromancy as it is practiced today.

Palmistry is a complex art. Far from the quick perusal of a hand, it requires an in-depth knowledge of both human nature and of the dozens and dozens of lines and symbols that may appear on the palm. This art is so complicated that many students soon abandon their studies. However, some major points of palmistry can be included here. The interested student should consult any of a number of books currently available for further information.

Most palmists make no claims that psychic powers are at work during a reading. They believe everything that needs to be revealed is right there on the palm. Although great familiarity with these signs is required, psychic awareness is not.

In brief, palmistry consists of two parts: the study of the shape of the hand, fingers, joints, nails and thumb, and of the markings and lines on the palm and wrists.

Both hands are read. An old saying, "The left hand is what we're born with; the right hand is what we make," perfectly sums up the difference between the two. The right hand is compared to the left hand to judge how we've lived our lives; the right hand reveals the present and future.

The Seven Types of Hands

As previously mentioned, the shape of the hand is as important as the markings found upon its palm. Briefly, the types are:

The elementary hand: A small, short hand, somewhat thick. The fingers are stubby; the palm is heavy. Such a person is usually a slow thinker, and may have no control over her or his emotions, which can lead to violent outbursts.

The square hand: This is what it sounds like—the palm is square, as are the tips of the fingers and the nails. A square hand indicates a level-headed person who is successful in business. These persons tend to be punctual, law-abiding, and not fanatical.

The philosophic hand: This is angular and long, usually with pronounced joints on the fingers, which also tend to be long. Such a hand indicates a person who is often wrapped in thought, who is sensitive and dignified. Lovers of mystery, they tend to be silent and secretive.

The spatulate hand: The palm is usually triangular shaped, and is far broader at either the base or below the fingers. The fingers themselves resemble spatulas, that is, they're broad and flat. Spatulate hands indicate a love of action, great independence, unconventionality, energy, and inventiveness. Originality is the key word.

The conic or artistic hand: A full hand, well-shaped, either rounded or cone-shaped. The tips of the fingers are slightly pointed. Persons with such hands are fine conversationalists, enjoy meeting new people, and are generous to others. They enjoy art in all its forms.

The psychic hand: This is slender and long, narrow and fragile looking, with extremely long fingers that taper to the nails. Persons with this hand are often dreamy and physically weak. They're quiet, gentle, and trust everyone. Impractical persons, they also often enjoy music.

The mixed hand: This is, obviously, a hand that mixes features of the other six types described above. Such persons are highly adaptable to all facets of life, but may wander about without real purpose. They may study a number of arts and pursue a variety of careers.

Once the type of hand has been determined, the palm is studied.

The Six Major Lines of the Hand

These are usually considered to be the most important when reading a palm, but other signs near or on them, as well as lesser lines, are all taken into consideration as a whole.

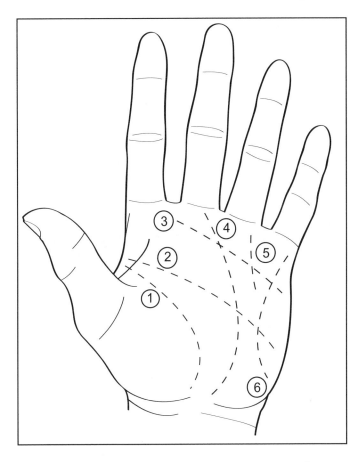

The Life line (1). Reveals health or sickness, as well as the year of death.

The Head line (2). Relates to intellectual capacity; can reveal mental illness.

The Heart line (3). Love and emotions. A line originating under the index finger indicates great affection. A line originating below the juncture of index and second fingers the emotions will be checked by practical matters. If the line begins below the second finger, a very sexual nature is indicated.

The Fate line (4). Relates to success or failure in worldly affairs; self-determination or external forces.

The Sun line (5). Creative energies and success.

The Intuition line (6). Sensuality, dreams, passions, great imagination. May indicate, by its appearance, a propensity for psychic awareness.

These are just the briefest glimpses into the mysteries of palmistry. A massive amount of published information is available on this topic.

20

The I Ching, or
Book of Changes

The I Ching is the most famed of all Chinese divination tools. The I Ching, or Book of Changes, consists of a group of sixty-four special symbols, known as hexagrams, together with their divinatory meanings, as well as commentaries and other ancillary information.

The I Ching is an elegant system of divination. Re-publication of the book during the late 1960s and early 1970s created intense interest in its use. It is consulted by a wide cross-section of individuals.

Some scholars claim that the I Ching wasn't used in antiquity to predict the future. Instead, it was thought to reveal the present situation. However, ancient records prove that this wasn't always the case. In the 600s and 500s B.C.E., the I Ching was consulted to determine such matters as the advisability of a marriage between two persons, the possibility of rain, and other questions regarding the future.

Scholars believe that the ancient practice of creating designs of six broken or unbroken lines (the hexagrams) dates back as early as 1000 B.C.E. We have no records of the earliest tools used to produce these series of lines, but a thousand years later yarrow stalks were favored.

Creating the Hexagram

This complex system of creating the hexagrams involved the use of fifty stalks. One stalk was immediately removed and set aside. The others were tossed onto a flat surface. The diviner divided the remaining stalks into two piles, and then removed the stalks from each in groups of four. The remaining number of stalks determined whether a broken or an unbroken line was indicated. The appropriate line was drawn on a piece of paper; the first such line was placed at the bottom. The entire procedure was repeated six times in all with each line being placed above the last, thus producing six lines.

This created the hexagram, for which there were sixty-four possible arrangements. In the earliest times, each hexa-gram was subject to a wide variety of interpretations. Eventually, a standardized set of interpretations was accepted by the state and was thereafter widely used. It is these interpretations that continue to be consulted today.

Since the I Ching is still used, and the yarrow stalk system of creating the hexagrams is rather time-consuming, a new method that uses three coins was created. These coins should be of the exact same weight and material, and should possess enough variety on each side so that it's readily apparent whether they've landed heads or tails up. Some use pennies; I prefer to use quarters.

The three coins are tossed onto a flat surface. Heads are given the numeric value of two; tails, the value of three. After tossing the coins, their values are added to determine the type of line to be drawn. When using three coins, there are only four possible combinations. These are two heads, one tail (4 + 3 = 7); one head, two tails (2 + 6 = 8); three heads (2 + 2 + 2 = 6); and three tails (3 + 3 + 3 = 9).

The number 6 for a throw indicates a broken line, 7 a solid line, 8 a broken line, and 9 a solid line. As with the yarrow stalks, the coins are tossed six times, and the hexagram is built up from the bottom line.

9 =
8 =
7 =
6 =

Reading the I Ching

Once this has been achieved, the book is consulted. Each hexagram is both named and numbered, which facilitates finding the appropriate information.

The symbolism and divinatory meaning of the hexagram is read in relation to the diviner's question. Many persons find that the I Ching is most useful in clarifying a present situation, or in determining whether she or he is living in harmony with personal objectives.

At times, the hexagram's meaning will be quite clear, though couched in symbolism. At other times, thought and reflection may be necessary to understand its message. The I Ching isn't an instant form of divination; it relies on the diviner to comprehend its meaning.

The I Ching chart on page 195 gives the Chinese names for the top and bottom trigrams. Read the top trigram first and then go down the chart until you see the name for the bottom trigram. This is keyed to the number of the hexagram and the name of the hexagram to consult for your future. For example, read the following hexagram:

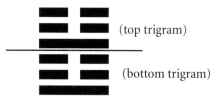

The top trigram is the Chinese name "Chên," and the bottom reads "Ch'ien." The place where the bottom and top trigram meet on the chart is number 34. There are two readings of this hexagram in the I Ching, one older at the beginning of the book, one newer at the end of the book. The Chinese name for hexagram 34 is "ta Chuang," which in English means "The Power of the Great."

Not only is the I Ching purposely obscure, but specific types of lines may point to other hexagrams. These "moving" lines are those created by three heads or three tails. A single line of a specific value in a specific location may also lead to further information. This information is clearly laid out in the I Ching itself.

A Sample Reading

Though this process is fairly simple, an example of an actual reading may serve to clarify the nature of this form of divination.

The question is asked: "Am I doing enough to assist other persons in my work?"

First throw: three tails = 9, a solid line

Second throw: two tails, one head = 8, a broken line

Third throw: two tails, one head = 8, a broken line

Fourth throw: two tails, one head = 8, a broken line

Fifth throw: three heads = 9, a solid line

Sixth throw: two tails, one head = 8, a broken line

Placed in the correct order, the hexagram looks like this:

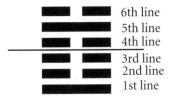

6th line
5th line
4th line
3rd line
2nd line
1st line

This creates the hexagram known as "Chun," which is numbered 3 in the I Ching.

The Book of Changes is consulted. In English, Chun has the meaning: "difficulty in the beginning." Symbolically, Chun represents a tiny blade of grass struggling to emerge from the earth. Once it has achieved this goal, it can freely grow without further obstacle; hence, "difficulty in the beginning."

This hexagram denotes a time of difficult growth. The diviner is encouraged to find helpers to rise above the current chaos. However, in the chaos itself lies order. It is up to the diviner to work through these difficulties. Success is assured if this is done.

Viewed in relation to the question, the answer seems fairly clear. The diviner is currently experiencing a time of difficulty. In order to fully help others with their lives, the diviner must not rely solely on the self, as this can be dangerous. She or he must seek the support and help of others. To avoid this would be to fail to achieve her or his goal.

Thus, the answer is no, but the objective can be attained by allowing others to lend support.

The I Ching's enormous popularity in both Asian and Western cultures points to its universal value as a tool for understanding our lives. It can be used by anyone who feels the need to consult the Book of Changes.

Trigrams

Upper → Lower ↓	Ch'ien ☰	Chên ☳	K'an ☵	Kên ☶	K'un ☷	Sun ☴	Li ☲	Tui ☱
Ch'ien ☰	1	34	5	26	11	9	14	43
Chên ☳	25	51	3	27	24	42	21	17
K'an ☵	6	40	29	4	7	59	64	47
Kên ☶	33	62	39	52	15	53	56	31
K'un ☷	12	16	8	23	2	20	35	45
Sun ☴	44	32	48	18	46	57	50	28
Li ☲	13	55	63	22	36	37	30	49
Tui ☱	10	54	60	41	19	61	38	58

21

The Future Is Now

In this age, when self-help books reach the top of the sales charts, it's apparent that we as humans are no longer content to live our lives without direction. We search for the perfect techniques to improve ourselves. We read books, attend seminars, and may spend time each day in pursuit of our quest. These measures are quite effective for some individuals. Others, however, realize that something is missing—they have a goal, and a map to reach that goal—but they're uncertain of the best route to take. They may lapse into despair and do nothing to improve their lives.

As we've seen, divination provides us with that vital information. It presents us with a view of the direction in which we're heading. By analyzing this information and applying it to our present lives, we can detour around unpleasant destinations and improve the quality of our lives.

This, and the knowledge that we can re-create our future lives before they occur, are the greatest lessons that divination has to offer. Divination can also assist us in planning events, ease the process of making difficult choices, provide advice and bring order into our lives.

As a tool designed to access otherwise unknowable information, divination can play a vital role in conforming our lives to our expectations, dreams and desires. It can assist us in learning the lessons that we haven't yet mastered, thus smoothing the path that we tread into the future.

Accepting responsibility for the state of our lives isn't an easy task. "How could this have happened?" we may ask in moments of crisis. Once we've accepted that we've created our present and future by past choices in action, we begin to lose the feeling of powerlessness over our lives. This spurs us toward living well today so that tomorrow won't present further avoidable challenges.

Divination can be seen as a friend who possesses great wisdom and knowledge. However, the information that we receive from its practice must be put to use if it is to be of any value.

This chapter's title presents a vitally important message. We usually consider the future as being a hazy possibility completely unconnected to the present. This is erroneous. The past, the present, and the future simultaneously exist in this moment, in this nanosecond. They don't consist of three separate compartments; they're one. Once we're aware of this fact we can utilize it to our advantage.

Tomorrow is but a heartbeat away. The illusion that we know as time may be useful, but only if we recognize its flexibility. We can stretch time and move within it.

The use of divination, then, can be for more than the simple satisfaction of our natural curiosity. It can provide invaluable information. Using the responses that we receive, we can build our lives into more positive, fulfilling experiences. The future is now.

Appendix 1

A Dictionary of Divinations

T his appendix lists some of the methods to which humans have turned to determine the future. They've
been gathered from all over the world and from all times,
and demonstrate that we have always desired to know what
lies ahead.

Divinations discussed at length elsewhere in the book
are give only cursory treatment here; the reader is invited
to consult the appropriate chapter (named in such cases)
for further information. Only those divinations that haven't
been fully described in the preceding chapters are here covered with any thoroughness.

Many of these divinations remain mysterious. The exact
techniques involved in the use of salt, for example, have
been lost. For others, conflicting information exists as to
the proper use of the tools and the methods of interpreting
the messages that they produce.

Some of these practices are cruel and barbaric, but they
were created in cruel and barbaric times. Life was incredibly short and uncertain, and persons used every means at

their disposal to determine the future. However, it's no accident that the most commonly used forms of divination today, even ones of antique origin, are those that require no sacrifice or bones. We've changed.

This list, though lengthy, is far from complete. Indeed, humans continue to create new methods of lifting the veil from the future, and will continue to do so as long as our species walks upon this planet and wonders about tomorrow.

Aeromancy: Divination by specific and deliberate observation of atmospheric phenomena, including clouds, storms, comets, winds, and other forces. See Chapter 10: Wind, Clouds, and Birds for more information.

Alectryomancy: Divination with roosters. Outdoors, a circle was created of small pieces of paper, each of which bore one of the letters of the alphabet. One kernel of dried corn was put on each of these letters. A white rooster was then placed in the center of the circle. The letters from which the rooster pecked the grain spelled out a message that pertained to the diviner's future. A most ancient form of divination and an aspect of ornithomancy.

Aleuromancy: Divination practiced with flour. Words and sentences stating possible futures were written on small slips of paper. Each piece of paper was rolled up in a ball of flour dough. The balls were then mixed thoroughly nine times and one was chosen. The chosen ball, when read, revealed the future. Apollo presided over this form of divination. The fortune cookie (an American invention—don't blame the Chinese) is a modern form of this ancient practice.

Alomancy: Salt as a tool of divination. Very little is known about this ancient method. Perhaps it was related to sand reading. See Chapter 17: Other Forms of Divination.

Alphitomancy: The use of wheat or barley in an oracular trial, the purpose of which was to discover a person guilty of some crime. The suspects were rounded up. Each was required to say, "If I am deceiving you, may this bread act upon me foul." A portion of barley or wheat bread was then served to each suspect. Those innocent of the crime would suffer no ill effects, while the guilty party would experience an attack of indigestion so painful that it was impossible to conceal it. (Sometimes the loaf was rubbed with vervain prior to being served. As a sacred herb, vervain could have been of assistance here.)

Amniomancy: Divination by examination of the caul that occasionally covers a child's face or head at birth. This revealed the child's future life.

Astragalomancy: A letter, word, or symbol was written on each of a dozen knuckle-bones. The bones (ancient precursors to dice) were thrown on the ground and the future was determined by their relative positions and by the symbols that lay face-up. Modern equivalent: cleromancy.

Austromancy: Divination from the winds. See Chapter 10: Wind, Clouds, and Birds for more information.

Axinomancy: Divination by means of an axe. Two methods were in common use. In the first, an axe was tossed into the air in an open area free of trees. If tossed correctly, the blade would stick into the ground. Prognostications were made from the direction in which the axe handle pointed and the amount of time it remained standing before falling to the ground. A second method is closely related to the first, but was only used to discover the presence of buried treasure. An axe head was heated in a fire until red hot. The axe was placed on the ground in the area where treasure might exist in such a way that the axe's sharp edge faced the sky. A round agate was then placed on the edge. If it remained there without moving, no treasure was in the area. If it fell, it would roll quickly away. This ritual was repeated two more times. If the agate rolled toward the same direction all three times, that was the most ideal place to dig, for the treasure was within thirty-one paces. If it rolled in a different direction each time, more searching was required. To find a thief, an axe was thrust into the ground with its handle pointing straight up. The group of people gathered for this oracle (which most assuredly included the thief's victim) danced around the axe in a ring until the axe's handle fell completely to the ground. The direction in which the axe pointed indicated the direction in which the thief should be sought. Axe divination was also used in some cultures to determine the most auspicious place for a woman to give birth.

Belomancy: Prognostications from arrows. A popular form of divination throughout the world, including Greece, Rome, and the Middle East. There are at least two methods: an arrow was shot straight up into the sky. The direction of the arrow's flight and the position in which it landed revealed the future. A second method consisted of shooting arrows at a rock and interpreting the markings the arrowheads made against its surface. This method existed among the Greeks, and still later among the Arabians. A similar form of divination was used in ancient Guatemala. When King Kicah Tanub was informed that white men had conquered Mexico and were heading for Guatemala, he immediately sent for four of his best diviners. The diviners shot arrows against a rock. Because the arrow heads left no markings on the rock, the diviners predicted the fall of Guatemala to the white men. They were quite correct. A totally different method of belomancy was used in ancient

Tibet. This consisted of placing two arrows point downward in a vessel. After an appropriate ritual, the arrows, by their seemingly miraculous movements, determined the future. In another form of belomancy potential future events were written or carved onto arrows. These were placed in a quiver, feathered ends up, and one was selected at random to determine the future.

Bibliomancy: A book was opened at random and the text revealed the future. Alternately, a pin was pushed into a book while closed; the book is opened, and the marked passage read. Any type of book was used, but many Christians used the Bible for this rather non-Christian practice. In ancient Greece, the works of Homer were preferred, as were those of Euripides. The Romans relied on Virgil. A variant on this practice is as follows: ask a yes or no question. Open a book at random, close your eyes, and bring your finger down on to a sentence. Count off the number of letters within the sentence, ignoring punctuation. If even, the answer is yes, if odd, no.

Botanomancy: Divination with plants. See Chapter 11: Plants and Herbs.

Capnomancy: Divination by smoke. See Chapter 9: Fire, Candles, Smoke, and Ash.

Catoptromancy: Divination through the use of mirrors. See Chapter 15: Mirrors.

Cartomancy: Divination through the use of regular playing cards or the tarot. For a discussion of the latter, see Chapter 18: Tarot.

Causmomancy: Divination by fire. See Chapter 9: Fire, Candles, Smoke, and Ash.

Cephalomancy: An ancient form of divination performed using a donkey's skull.

Ceraunoscopy: Divination performed by observation of the wind: its strength, direction, or absence. Whirlwinds were also observed. See Chapter 10: Wind, Clouds, and Birds.

Ceroscopy: Divination with molten wax. The wax is melted in a brass pot over a low fire and is then slowly poured into a vessel filled with cold water. The symbols and shapes created as the wax hardens in the water are read for omens of the future. This method is still in use.

Cheiromancy: (Also known as palmistry.) Divination by studying the marks and lines of the hands, as well as their shapes, and the condition of the fingernails, to determine a person's future and character. See Chapter 19: Palmistry.

Cleidomancy: Divination through the use of a key suspended from a thread and held between the thumb and forefinger. The key was lowered into a glass and a question asked. The key would knock against the glass; one knock meant yes, two meant no. Similar to dactylomancy. Some authorities state that this was best performed while the sun and moon are in Virgo, which would greatly limit its usefulness.

Cleromancy: The casting of lots; also, divination through the use of dice. See Chapter 12: Casting the Lots.

Coscinomancy: Divination with a sieve and tongs or shears. An old method of discovering the identity of a person responsible for a crime.

Critomancy: Divination by food. Usually associated in ancient times with the food left or burnt on altars for offerings, especially cakes, which were a preferred sacrifice. A modern form consists of baking small objects (thimbles, whole walnuts, rings and so on) into cakes or pancakes, or inserting them into mashed potatoes. The person who is served the piece containing the charm determines her or his future according to its traditional meaning. Rings mean marriage, silver coins mean money, and walnuts mean health. This practice dates back to at least 1778 in England.

Cromniomancy: Divination with onions. See Chapter 11: Plants and Herbs.

Crystallomancy: Divination through the use of a sphere of quartz crystal. See Chapter 13: Crystal Gazing.

Cyclomancy: Divination through the consultation of a turning wheel; probably the forerunner of the famous gambling tool, the wheel of fortune.

Dactylomancy: Divination with rings. See Chapter 19: Other Forms of Divination.

Daphnomancy: Divination with laurel (bay) leaves or branches. See Chapter 11: Plants and Herbs.

Dendromancy: Divination through the use of oak and mistletoe.

Elaeomancy: A form of water gazing in which a liquid surface is studied to present the future. See Chapter 8: Water.

Extispicy: Divination by observation of the entrails of sacrificed animals. This ancient art has, fortunately, long died out in most cultures.

Geomancy: Divination by the swelling, noises, and movement of the earth. Also, studying cracks made in dried mud by the sun. Later, an elaborate form was created, using dots made at random to determine the future. These dots were originally created in the earth; hence it was known as geomancy as well.

Gyromancy: A curious form of divination in which several persons whirled around in circles within a large ring, the perimeter of which was marked with the letters of the alphabet. As the dancers became dizzy, they would occasionally step upon one or more of the letters, and it was from the words thus formed that the future was divined.

Hepatoscopy: Divination by examination of the liver of a sacrificed animal. Practiced in ancient Greece, Rome, Babylon, and elsewhere in the ancient world.

Hippomancy: Divination with horses. The ancient Celts kept special white horses in sacred groves of trees. During sacred processions, the horses followed the lead cart, and the future was divined by their behavior. A second method was in use by the ancient Germans, who kept sacred horses in some of their temples. If, while leaving the temple to carry warriors into battle, the horse's left forefoot was the first to step outside the holy precincts, the warriors were convinced that they would not be successful, and so would cancel the planned surprise attack.

Hydromancy: Divination by water. See Chapter 8: Water.

Lampadomancy: Omens of the future obtained by observing flickering torches. If the torch's flame formed itself into one point, the signs were favorable; into two points, unfavorable, while three points on the same torch was considered the most auspicious of all. If the flame bent, the healthy would become sick; if the torch was suddenly extinguished for no apparent reason, disaster was in the offing.

Lecanomancy: The observation of oil dropped onto water. See Chapter 17: Other Forms of Divination.

Libanomancy: The observation of smoke rising from incense. See Chapter 9: Fire, Candles, Smoke, and Ash.

Lithomancy: An obscure form of divination that used polished (not faceted) stones to create predictions of the future. Little is known about this ancient art, but it seems likely that large, gleaming stones could have been used in the same manner as was the crystal ball. Also, a specific type of stone, described as being black and finely veined with another mineral, was held to the eyes and the future divined by reading the lines on the stone's surface.

Lychnomancy: Anciently, divination from the flame of an oil lamp. Today, another name for divination with candles. See Chapter 9: Fire, Candles, Smoke, and Ash.

Margaritomancy: Divination with pearls. See Chapter 17: Other Forms of Divination.

Metoscopy: Character divination by the observation of a person's forehead.

Molybdomancy: Divination with lead. A small quantity of the heavy metal was melted and poured quickly into a bowl of water. The future was read in the shapes thus created. (A similar method consisted of pouring the molten lead onto the ground and, after it had cooled, observing its forms.) This form of divination can produce the most unusual shapes.

Myomancy: A curious form in which the squeaks of mice, together with the damage that they cause, are interpreted as omens of the future.

Nephelomancy: Divination from the appearance of clouds. See Chapter 10: Wind, Clouds, and Birds.

Numerology: Character divination through the study of numbers related to the person in question.

Oinomancy: (Also Oenomancy) Gazing into a goblet filled with dark red wine. See Chapter 8: Water.

Ololygmancy: Predictions based on the howling of dogs. These are usually considered to be negative omens.

Oneiromancy: The interpretation of dreams. This was once highly favored, as dreams, when requested, were believed to have been sent by the deities.

Onomancy: Divination based on names. Related to numerology.

Onychomancy: Divination by gazing at highly polished fingernails, onychomancy was usually performed outdoors in full sunshine. The preferred owner of the fingernails was a young boy who was "unpolluted" (i.e., who had yet to reach puberty.)

Oomantia: Divination through the inspection of egg whites. See Chapter 17: Other Forms of Divination.

Ornithomancy: Divination through the observation of birds. See Chapter 10: Wind, Clouds, and Birds.

Ovomancy: Another term for oomantia.

Pegomancy: Divination by the sounds, murmurings, and appearance of water flowing from a fountain. In Rome, fountains were sometimes merely springs around which small structures were built. Alternately, they were similar to our versions, and were fed by water running down from the mountains in aqueducts. The pressure of the water as it reached the fountain caused it to spray up into the air. As anyone who has ever listened to a fountain knows, the water falling into the basin produces sounds which, indeed, could be used to divine the future.

Pessomancy: Divination with pebbles. See Chapter 12: Casting the Lots.

Plastromancy: Divination through the use of turtle's shells. An ancient Chinese art. Another practice may have been used by the murderous dictator of Uganda, Idi Amin. He apparently consulted a turtle. By its responses, the creature predicted the collapse of Amin's empire. Characteristically. Amin had the offensive turtle made into soup as punishment. The turtle, though, had the last laugh; Amin did fall as predicted. (This story may be apocryphal.)

Psephoman: See Cleromancy.

Phyllorhodomancy: Divination by rose leaves. See Chapter 11: Plants and Herbs.

Physiognomy: Character divination from the appearance of the human body, including the forehead, the position of moles, facial types, and so on.

Pyromancy: Divination by fire, sometimes in sacrifice. See Chapter 9: Fire, Candles, Smoke, and Ash.

Rhabdomancy: The use of specially prepared branches or magic wands to uncover hidden treasures (gold, oil, water, etc.). Pliny wrote that it was in use by the Etruscans, forerunners of the Romans, to find hidden sources of water. By the fifteenth century it had been imported from Germany to England. It has always been used in China. The modern form is known as dowsing or water witching. A forked branch (or a specially designed, Y-shaped metal tool) is held lightly in the hands, palms upward. The area is traversed. The rod will dramatically dip downward when the diviner passes over the desired object. Rods of this type are made of a variety of trees, including peach, willow, blackthorn, and hazel, considered to produce the best results. The wood of the elder is never used for water-witching. Dowsing organizations exist in the United States, and many dowsers are hired by oil companies to seek out hidden deposits of oil. Similarly, farmers and other persons living in rural areas often consult a "water witch" (the term has no connection with Witchcraft or magic) when searching for the most likely spot to dig a new well. Exceptional water-witches are usually highly sought and well paid, but they're rare. A study revealed that only one out of ten persons possess this ability to any great degree, and even this talent may vary according to the dowser's health. This art has never been fully explained. One fact, however, remains clear—it works.

Rhapsodomancy: A form of oracle wherein a book of poetry is opened at random and the passage that immediately reveals itself before the eyes is searched for divinatory clues. Another name for bibliomancy.

Scyphomancy: Divination with the use of cups or vases. See Chapter 8: Water.

Sideromancy: Divination from the burning of straws. See Chapter 9: Fire, Candles, Smoke, and Ash.

Spodomancy: Divination through the use of ashes. See Chapter 9: Fire, Candles, Smoke, and Ash.

Stolisomancy: Divination from the observance of the act of dressing. A curious historic example: one morning while he was being dressed by his valet, the servant buckled Augustus Caesar's right sandal to his left foot. Augustus knew then that a military revolt would occur that day. Putting on clothing inside out and buttoning shirts and dresses incorrectly are some common stolisomantic omens.

Sycomancy: Divination with leaves, often those of fig trees. See Chapter 11: Plants and Herbs.

Tasseography: Divination by the observation of tea leaves left in the bottom of a cup after the tea has been drunk. The wet tea leaves clinging to the sides of a cup are read with symbolic thought. This can be a highly effective method of divination.

Tephramancy: Use of wind or breath in divination. See Chapter 10: Wind, Clouds, and Birds.

Tiromancy (also known as tyromancy)**:** A curious form of divination involving cheese. It may have consisted of observing milk as it curdled. The curds so formed might have been interpreted with symbolic thought. (Cheese has been made throughout history.) A curious modern form of tiromancy was recorded by a folklore specialist in Cleveland in 1960. On New Year's Eve, cut a thick slice from a wheel of Swiss cheese. Study the holes in it on one side only. If there are an odd number, the coming year will be unfavorable. If an even number, favorable. Additionally, a preponderance of small holes mean minor luck or pains, while a greater number of large holes indicate major events.

Xylomancy: Divination with wood. A question was asked while walking in the forest. The ground was watched. Any pieces of wood found lying there were interpreted according to their shape, type (if known), and so on.

Appendix 2

Unusual Forms of Divination

For a variety of reasons, most of the information presented in this appendix isn't recommended for actual use. Some require bones; others tools that are virtually unobtainable in our society. Still others are potentially hazardous or simply impractical.

In spite of these facts, a book of traditional methods of divination would be incomplete without at least cursory explanations of some of the strange and wonderful methods that humans have used to peer into the future.

This information is arranged here in no particular order.

Mutton Shoulder Bone

Using the shoulder bone of a lamb is a survivor of earlier practices, when sacrificed animals were examined for signs of the future. At least in its more modern forms, this divination was only practiced after the lamb had been cooked and eaten.

It was performed for distinct purposes. The first determined the sex of an unborn child. A mutton shoulder bone was cleaned of all meat after dinner. It was then held in the fire until it was well scorched on its thinnest part. The thumbs were forced through this area and a string was passed through them. This string was knotted and hung on the back door. If, other than a family member, the first person to enter through this door after the rite was a male, the child will be a boy. If a woman, a girl.

Another form consisted of the examination of the cracks created by scorching the bone in a fire, and inspection of the cleaned (but not burned) blade for spots, which were thought to predict disaster or death. This last technique was common in Scotland. Pulling a wishbone is a contemporary survivor of the ancient practice of turning to bones for divinatory purposes.

The Snail

In some cultures, corn meal was evenly spread on the ground. A living snail was put on the meal. The patterns created by the snail's slime as it moved off the meal predicted the future.

Crabs

Crabs have been used in two unique ways. In the first, a crab was placed in a vessel of water. The movement of the crab as it attempted to escape predicted the future success or failure of a specific event. Alternately, a bowl filled with damp sand was used. The markings from the crab's many feet on the sand were read like tea leaves.

Termites

The Azande of Africa ingeniously use these destructive creatures to answer questions. The diviner cut two sticks from two different kinds of wood and took them to a termite mound (the size of some of these dwarf the height of humans). The diviner spoke to the termites, asking that they eat one of the sticks if the answer is yes, the other if the answer is no. She or he placed the sticks in a hole in the mound, filled in the space around them, and returned the next day to determine the termite's answer.

Various Forms of Lot Casting

In West Africa, sixteen palm kernels are thrown, in pairs, onto the ground. Their relative positions reveal the future. Some cultures threw grain into the air and read the patterns created when it hit the ground. Shamans in Madagascar drew circles on the ground. Seeds were then tossed and, according to the patterns they created and the circles in which they landed, the future was predicted.

Other forms of lot casting include that used by the Bantu of South Africa. Four bones, representing an old man, a old woman, a young man, and a young woman, are scattered on the ground to form a pattern, which is then read. Other cultures used the bones of many specific types of creatures (baboon, impala, wart hog, etc.) in a similar method. Sometimes these were mixed with shells, stones, and other objects.

Rubbing Boards

The Azande, in what was once the Belgian Congo, used a curious tool known as a rubbing board. This was an object that resembled a table with two legs. The juice of a fruit was smeared over the table's top, and a second piece of wood was placed on this. A question was asked. If the top moved smoothly over the bottom, the answer was yes. If the two pieces of wood stuck together, no.

Observation of Animals

Aside from those methods listed above, many others exist. Fish were placed in tanks of water and the future determined by their movements. A pit of snakes was also used in the same manner. Among the Aztecs, snakes pointed out a thief among many others; the Haidas of British Columbia employed mice for a similar purpose.

Glossary of Related Terms

Augur: One who performs divination. Originally, this term referred in Rome to the practices of a special class of diviners who specialized in the examination of omens.

Augury: Any form of divination.

Auspices: Specifically, the observation of the actions of birds to foretell the future. More generally, any form of divination.

Binary Response: A yes or no answer to a question obtained through divination.

Character Divination: The practice of using both natural and artificial tools in order to determine a person's character. These methods include palmistry, astrology, physiognomy (study of the human body), phrenology (reading the bumps on the head), numerology (the study of numbers of importance in a person's life), and others. This is a lesser branch of the divinatory arts, but the one most widely known to the general public.

Countercheck: A second divination performed to ascertain the veracity of the first one. It developed in ancient times.

Divination: The art of discovering the past, present, or future through consultation of tools or by the observation of natural phenomena. This is a deliberate art; it can't happen spontaneously. It's little understood today by nonpractitioners, and has been virulently denounced by certain religious organizations from a gross misunderstanding of the practice. Divination is not a form of magic; it is a means of gaining information through other than the five senses.

Divinatory Response: The answer or advice produced through divination.

Diviner: One who utilizes specific rites with the goal of obtaining information concerning the past, present, or future.

Energy Waves: See Waves of Energy.

Forecast: A prediction concerning the future. Today, forecasts made by television weather reporters are the most widely known form. The common lack of accuracy in weather reporting reflects not inexperience by the forecaster, but the constant change that surrounds the weather. Similarly, diviners must deal with altering waves of energy when determining the shape of the future.

Fortunetelling: A somewhat discredited term usually related to specific types of character reading. Little used by diviners themselves.

Gazing: The art of peering into clear objects, into water or at reflective surfaces in order to divine the future. This is a world-wide practice. Some popular forms include catoptromancy, crystallomancy, hydromancy, onychomancy, and so on. Also known as scrying or skrying. In most forms that utilize pools or other vessels of water, the images are seen within the liquid itself; they're not thought to be created by the mind. Some argue that gazing contacts the subconscious mind, but this is only partially true: it stimulates the sub-conscious mind so that it can interpret the symbols, not create them.

Omen: A sign of the future as revealed by the observance of accidental phenomena. Meetings with birds, clouds hanging over a house, the actions of animals, especially cats and dogs, knives being crossed, plants withering or flourishing are some popular omens. Many omens of this type possess ancient histories. Hundreds are listed in old Babylonian and Assyrian texts. Observation of omens isn't a form of divination unless the diviner requests that they appear within a certain time frame and in a specific setting.

Oracle: Generally speaking, a person who, possessed by the divine, utters prophecies from the deities. Also a temple where this activity occurs. The oracle at Delphi is perhaps the most famous Western example, but such temples were to be found throughout the classical world. In this book I occasionally use the word in reference to specific types of divination. However, true oracles don't perform divination.

Presage: A sign of the future. A divinatory response.

Prognostication: A fancy term for a response received during divination.

Prophecy: Technically speaking, a message from a deity received by an oracle. More loosely, responses received during divination.

Prophet: One who experiences prophecy.

Psychic: A person who naturally receives information from other than commonly accepted means of communication. Such individuals usually have no need to rely on divination, as they have an alternative—psychic awareness. Diviners needn't be psychic to gain accurate responses. Psychism is a function of the subconscious mind.

Reading: An alternate term for a rite of divination.

Response: See Divinatory Response.

Seer: Occasionally used in place of psychic or diviner.

Skryer: One who gazes.

Selective Response: In some forms of divination, a question is answered by the selection of a specific answer, usually written on paper, on leaves, or carved on to sticks, and so on. This form is highly popular in that it provides immediate and direct answers, but is limited to responding only within the range of choices provided.

Show Stone: A crystal sphere or black obsidian mirror used in gazing.

Soothsayer: Today used in a derogatory manner to describe diviners. Once used to describe those who said the "sooth" (truth), it has been largely discredited.

Sortilege: Generally, the act of foretelling the future by the casting of lots. Probably first formalized in ancient Sumer (circa 3000 B.C.E.), it remains in common use in most of the world. Tools involved in this practice include twigs, sticks, pebbles, coins, peas, seeds, beans of various colors, shells, dice, bones, stalks, dried corn, eggs, betel nuts, and staves. Examples include cleromancy and pessomancy.

Specularii: In ancient Rome, those who read mirrors for the purpose of divination.

Speculum: A mirror or another similar object used as a focal point during gazing.

Subconscious Mind: A convenient term that describes those aspects of the consciousness at work when we sleep, dream, daydream, are creative or otherwise use our minds in other than normal ways. During waking hours, the conscious mind is largely at work. During sleep, the subconscious rises to ascendancy. Many believe that not only does the subconscious mind receive information from nonphysical sources (psychic signals), it also transmit these banks of information to our conscious minds through dreams and intuition. The subconscious mind plays an active role in the interpretation of symbolic responses received during divination, but is not the ultimate source of these predictions.

Symbolic Response: In divination, answers to posed questions that appear in symbolic form. The imagery is studied to reveal the future using symbolic thought.

Symbolic Thought: A necessary adjunct to the practices of what may be termed symbolic forms of divination. The symbols received are interpreted according to the diviner's personal symbolic system.

Waves of Energy: In this book's context, our past, immediate, and future actions radiate energy. This energy, visualized as waves (much like sound waves), continues to travel with us and ahead of us throughout our lives. Thus it can greatly affect our future. Cause and effect plays a vital role here: decisions made today alter the waves that we'll confront tomorrow (or next year). To change an ominous future, it's necessary to change these waves through positive thought and action.

Annotated Bibliography

I've relied upon extensive experience in using divination while writing this book. I've also researched the subject to confirm inner knowledge, expand specific information on certain forms, and to discover methods to which I'd never been introduced by my teachers. This select bibliography lists some of the most useful of these sources.

The inclusion of a book here shouldn't be viewed as a wholehearted recommendation. I have strong disagreements with many of these works, and reject the vast majority of definitions of divination presented within them. Many include detailed instructions for divination with bones or livers, raising the dead and other unsavory practices. Some include Christian-flavored techniques. Read with discretion.

You'll notice that this list is largely composed of books concerned with folklore, folk customs, and superstitions. These are the treasure houses of traditional forms of divination. Books bearing the words "divination" or "fortune-telling" in their titles are usually limited to discussing a few well-known forms. In these wondrous works, however, no such boundaries exist. Wishbones, birds, colors, four-leaf clovers, numbers, fingernail spots, divinatory dreams, gazings, omens—they're all here in these invaluable records of the survival of ancient divinations.

Abbott, C. F. *Macedonian Folklore.* 1893. Reprint. Chicago: Argonaut, 1969. Minor divinations, such as determining a future love.

Agrippa, Henry Cornelius. *Three Books of Occult Philosophy.* 1533. First English edition, 1651. Reprint. Chthonios Books, 1986. Agrippa includes several techniques of divination that were in use in the early 1500s.

Beckwith, Martha. *Hawaiian Mythology.* Honolulu, Hawaii: University Press of Hawaii, 1979. Various forms of divination used in premissionary Hawaii.

Brelsford, Vernon. *Superstitious Survivals.* New York: Robert M. McBryde, 1959. A section concerning rhabdomancy is rather interesting.

Butler, Bill. *Dictionary of the Tarot.* New York: Schocken Books, 1975. An unusual work. Butler provides summaries of each card's meaning according to a wide number of authors. The range of accepted interpretations is quite curious.

Butler, W. E. *How to Develop Clairvoyance.* New York: Weiser, 1968. Though the author seems to consider the use of psychic abilities as divination, this is still a handy, short guide to a subject of related interest. He includes several techniques for creating unusual gazing tools, such as a sand disc and a black mirror.

Chappell, Helen. *The Waxing Moon: A Gentle Guide to Magick.* New York: Links Books, 1973. Chapter 3 discusses several methods of divination.

Cheiro (Count Louis Harmony). *Cheiro's Complete Palmistry.* Edited by Robert M. Okene. New York: Dell, 1969. A compilation of several of Cheiro's rare and out of print works. A fine introduction.

Christian, Paul. *The History and Practice of Magic.* New York: Citadel, 1969. Divination with rings, dowsing, and other forms.

Clough, Nigel R. *How to Make and Use Magic Mirrors.* New York: Samuel Weiser, 1977. A curious work dedicated to the construction and utilization of magic mirrors for divinatory and other purposes.

Coffin, Tristram P., and Henning Cohen, editors. *Folklore in America.* Garden City, N.Y.: Anchor Books, 1970. A few divinatory rites are included in this work, gathered from living informants.

Contenau, Georges. *Everyday Life in Babylon and Assyria.* New York: Norton, 1966. Babylonian divination.

Cunningham, Scott. *Earth Power: Techniques of Natural Magic.* St. Paul: Llewellyn, 1983. A wide variety of natural forms of divination.

———. *Sacred Sleep: Dreams and the Divine.* Freedom, Calif.: The Crossing Press, 1992. Provoked dreams in the ancient world; theories regarding dreams; dream interpretation.

De Lys, Claudia. *A Treasury of American Superstitions.* New York: Philosophical Library, 1948. Water lore, stars, bird, and much else of interest.

de Vere, M. Schele. *Modern Magic.* New York: Putnam's and Sons, 1873. A short explication of dowsing; many examples of fulfilled prophecies and divinatory warnings. A fascinating early book by a true disbeliever.

Ferm, Vergilius. *A Brief Dictionary of American Superstitions.* New York: Philosophical Library, 1959. Several forms of fortunetelling are included in this very brief compendium.

Fernie, William T. *The Occult and Curative Powers of Precious Stones.* 1907. Reprint. New York: Harper & Row, 1973. Contains an in-depth discussion of crystal gazing.

Friend, Hilderic. *Flower Lore.* 1884. Reprint. Rockport, Mass.: Para Research, 1981. Divinations with flowers, rhabdomancy, weather omens from plants. A fine collection of all types of flower and plant folklore.

Gleadow, Rupert. *The Origin of the Zodiac.* New York: Castle Books, 1968. Discusses the Babylonian origins of astrology, as well as the influence of other early cultures in perfecting the system.

Green, Marian. *The Elements of Natural Magic.* Longmead, England: Element Books, 1989. Contains some suggestions for performing hydromancy.

Guiley, Rosemary Ellen. *The Encyclopedia of Witches and Witchcraft.* New York: Facts on File, 1989. Many techniques of divination are included in this work, which is far broader in scope that the title may indicate.

Haining, Peter. *Superstitions.* London: Sidgwick and Jackson Ltd, 1979. Omens involving daily happenings and animals.

Hand, Wayland, Anna Casetta, and Sondra B. Theiderman, editors. *Popular Beliefs and Superstitions: A Compendium of American Folklore.* Three volumes. Boston: G. K. Hall, 1981. This work, which consists of over 35,000 individually numbered entries, is based on extensive field research conducted throughout Ohio during this century. It contains a wealth of simple folk rites. Divinations are found everywhere, especially those involved with determining love and the weather. Highly recommended.

Harley, Rev. Timothy. *Moon Lore.* 1885. Reprint. Rutland, Ver.: Charles E. Tuttle Co., 1970. What else? A book about moon lore.

Hooke, S. H. *Babylonian and Assyrian Religion.* Norman, Okla.: The University of Oklahoma Press, 1963. Divination in Babylon and Assyria; diviners; oil reading.

Howells, William. *The Heathens.* Garden City, N.J.: Doubleday, 1956. Lot casting, birds, unusual forms of divination.

Jayne, Walter Addison. *The Healing Gods of Ancient Civilizations.* New Hyde Park, N.Y.: University Books, 1962. Divination in Babylon and in many other Mesopotamian and early European cultures.

Kaplan, Stuart R. *Tarot Classic.* New York: Grossett and Dunlap, 1972. A fine introduction to the Tarot.

Kennedy, Crawford Q. *The Divination Handbook.* New York: Signet, 1990. A collection of short articles detailing many forms of divination. This author believes that all divination actually contacts the subconscious mind. How he justifies this is unclear, for he includes several techniques that create binary responses over which the subconscious mind can have no direct or indirect control. Still, it's a fine collection.

Kilpatrick, Jack Frederick, and Anna Gritts Kilpatrick. *Notebook of a Cherokee Shaman.* Washington D.C.: Smithsonian Institution Press, 1970. Includes post-European contact methods of divination used by the Cherokee, techniques with needles and stones.

King, Francis and Stephen Skinner. *Techniques of High Magic.* New York: Destiny Books, 1976. Includes an interesting section titled "Divination as Magic."

Kittredge, George Lyman. *Witchcraft in Old and New England.* New York: Russell and Russell, 1956. Various forms of

divination current in England from the tenth to the sixteenth centuries, mostly gleaned from civil trial records.
Many mentions of the use of mirrors to discover the
identity of thieves. Simultaneously fascinating and grim:
many of those so charged were executed for the crime of
practicing divination.

Lasne, Sophie and Andre Pascal Gaultier. *A Dictionary of
Superstitions.* Englewood Cliffs, N.J.: Prentice-Hall, 1984.
Translated from the French, this book contains information
concerning animals, the weather, days of the lunar months,
and much else of interest.

Lawson, John Cuthbert. *Modern Greek Folklore and Ancient
Greek Religion.* New Hyde Park, N.Y.: University Books,
1964. Divination in both ancient and modern Greece,
showing the survival of ancient forms into this century.

Lee, Albert. *Weather Wisdom: Being an Illustrated Practical Vol-
ume Wherein is Contained Unique Compilation and Analysis
of the Facts and Folklore of Natural Weather Prediction.* Garden City, N.Y.: Doubleday, 1976. An invaluable storehouse
of natural methods of weather predictions, including explanations of why so many them are accurate.

Leek, Sybil. *The Sybil Leek Book of Fortune Telling.* New York:
Collier, 1969. A charming introduction to several fortunetelling techniques, well sprinkled with the author's personal experiences.

Legge, Jame. *I Ching: Book of Changes.* N.p., n.d. One of the
earliest English translations of the I Ching. Also discusses
tortoiseshell divination among the ancient Chinese.

Lewisohn, Richard. *Science, Prophecies and Prediction.* New
York: Harper, 1961. A difficult book; the author's skepti-
cism overshadows the material that he presents within it.

He'll mention every unfulfilled prophecy, but ignores those that came true, even those recorded in history books. However, he does include some unusual theories regarding the manner in which divination reveals the future. No practical instructions are included.

Loewe, Michael, and Carmen Blacker, editors. *Oracles and Divination*. Boulder, Colo.: Shambhala, 1981. Divination throughout the ancient world, including Tibet, China, Greece and Rome, and ancient Germany. A fascinating account of this ancient art by a number of recognized experts. Absolutely indispensable.

Maple, Eric. *The Magic of Perfume: Aromatics and their Esoteric Significance.* New York: Weiser, 1973. Divination with bay leaves.

McBride, L. R. *The Kahuna: Versatile Mystics of Old Hawaii.* Hilo, Hawaii: The Petroglyph Press, 1972. Weather observation in pre-missionary Hawaii.

Miall, Agnes M. *The Book of Fortune Telling.* London: Hamlyn, 1972. Popular forms of character divination as well as a few other techniques.

Morrison, Lillian, editor and compiler. *Touch Blue Your Wish Will Come True.* New York: Thomas Y. Crowell Company, 1958. An enchanting collection of folk rhymes, many of which preserve old methods of divination. Includes love, moon lore and the stars.

Murdock, George Peter. *Our Primitive Contemporaries.* New York: The Macmillan Co., 1934. Divination among pretechnological cultures.

Oates, Joan. *Babylon*. London: Thames and Hudson, 1979. Divination in Babylon, omens, theories regarding divination in that ancient culture.

Opie, Iona, and Moira Tatem, editors. *A Dictionary of Super-stitions.* Oxford: Oxford University Press, 1989. Egg divinations, divination of future spouse.

Oppenheim, A. Leo. *Ancient Mesopotamia: Portrait of a Dead Civilization.* Chicago: University of Chicago Press, 1977. Babylonian divination; general theories of divination.

Paulsen, Kathryn. *The Complete Book of Witchcraft and Magic.* New York: Signet, 1980. A short dictionary of various forms of divination is included in this curious work.

Pelton, Robert W. *Your Future, Your Fortune.* Greenwich, Conn.: Fawcett, 1973. Several systems of divination are discussed in this introductory work.

Pepper, Elizabeth and John Wilcox. *The Witches' Almanac.* New York: Grosset & Dunlap. Aries 1971 to Pisces 1972, Aries 1979 to Pisces 1980, and other issues. Fire gazing; divination with apples, and all manner of similar wonders.

Peschel, Lisa. *A Practical Guide to the Runes: Their Uses in Divination and Magick*. St. Paul: Llewellyn, 1989. A guide to runic divination.

Poinsot, M. C. *The Encyclopedia of Occult Sciences.* New York: Robert M. Mcbride and Company, 1939. Divinatory mirrors.

Radford, Edwin and Mona A. *Encyclopedia of Superstitions.* New York: Philosophical Library 1949. A wide array of British folk divinations.

Randolph, Vance. *Ozark Superstitions.* New York: Columbia University Press, 1947. Several love divinations; mirrors.

Ronner, John. *Seeing the Future.* Oxford, Ala.: Mamre Press, 1990. A curious work. Most of the information related pertains to historic prophecies, but a short section included here discusses true divination. The author also presents some musings regarding the nature of time.

Schmidt, Phillip. *Superstition and Magic.* Westminster, Mary.: The Newman Press, 1963. German laws against divination in the 700s.

Shah, Sirdar Ikbal Ali. *Occultism: Its Theory and Practice.* New York: Castle Books, n.d. Several forms of divination are discussed in this unusual work, as well as colors and birds.

Showers, Paul. *Fortune Telling for Fun and Popularity.* New York: The New Home Library, 1942. Popular forms of divination; the book treats it as a game that will enhance any party. Still, some of the information is sound. The last chapter, "The Psychology of Fortune Telling," advises the reader to use psychology and observation to enhance a reading. A rather peculiar book.

Spence, Lewis. *An Encyclopedia of Occultism.* New Hyde Park New Jersey: University Books, 1960. Many articles on divination can be found in this comprehensive collection of occult practices and beliefs. Though Spence has often been criticized for going off the deep end in the presentation of his theories, the divinatory information here is sound.

Strachen, Francoise, et al. *The Fortune Tellers: Unlocking the Doors to Hidden Truths.* New York: Black Watch, 1974. Contains a curious purification ritual to be used before divination, together with articles on various well-known aspects of divination.

Thompson, C. J. S. *The Hand of Destiny: Folklore and Superstition for Everyday Life.* New York: Bell, 1989. Contains a wide variety of European divinations.

———. *The Mysteries and Secrets of Magic.* New York: Causeway Books, 1973. Chapter 14 discusses a variety of divinatory techniques; chapter 15 examines crystal gazing.

Tyson, Donald. *Rune Magic.* New York: Llewellyn, 1989. Chapter 10 discusses divination in general and the nature of time and chapter 11 provides detailed instructions for casting the runes.

Vinci, Leo. *The Book of Practical Candle Magic.* Wellingborough, England: The Aquarian Press, 1983. A short section discusses candle divination.

Waite, Arthur Edward. *The Pictorial Key to the Tarot.* 1910. Reprint. New York: Weiser, 1980. A basic Tarot text.

Waring, Phillipa. *A Dictionary of Omens and Superstitions.* New York: Ballantine, 1079. Many articles concerning divination are included in this work.

Weinstein, Marion. *Positive Magic: Occult Self-Help.* Custer, Wash.: Phoenix, 1981. A fine introduction to the I Ching is included in this classic work.

Wellman, Alice. *Spirit Magic.* New York: Berkeley, 1973. Much discussion of spirit possession, visions, and other phenomena in many cultures. Includes a short and valuable section on divinatory techniques. A unique work.

Wilhelm, Richard. *The I Ching or Book of Changes.* Translated into English by Cary F. Baynes. 1950. Reprint. Princeton: Princeton University Press, 1990. The finest translation of the I Ching available in English. Quite literally, the only book on the subject that anyone will ever need. Beware of other editions.

Winstead, Richard. *The Malay Magician.* Singapore: Oxford University press, 1985. Oil divination and other forms in use in Malaysia.

Index

A

aeromancy, 93, 200
  see also clouds, wind
animals, 6, 14, 16–17, 43–44,
  75, 112, 207, 215, 218, 221
  behavior, 6, 16–17, 23, 26,
    29, 49, 64–65, 75, 97, 208
  sacrifice of, 14, 23
  see also extispicy
ashes, 92, 212
astrology, 18–19, 139, 142,
  219
  horoscope, 19
  moon, 18–19, 26, 37, 58–59,
    76, 104
  planets, 18–19, 37
  stars, 6, 17, 19, 59
    comet, 139–140
    North Star (Sirius), 139
    shooting stars, 139–140
      see also meteorites
  sun, 83, 107
  zodiac, 18–19
austromancy, 93, 203
  see also wind

B

bibliomancy, 59, 205, 212
birds, 6, 14, 17, 22, 26, 29, 59,
  93, 95–102, 150, 202–203,
  206, 209–210, 213, 219, 221
  chickens, 22
Book of Changes, 189, 191,
  193–195
  see I Ching
botanomancy, 103, 205
  see also plants and herbs

C

Caesar, Julius, 22, 87
candles, 16, 59, 83–89, 91–92,
  104, 138, 205, 208–209,
  211–212
capnomancy, 90–91, 205
  see also smoke
cartomancy, 33, 205
casting of lots, 18, 26, 59,
  111–113, 115, 117, 206, 222
  see also dice, stones
  wooden lots, 117
catoptromancy, 203, 220
  see also mirrors